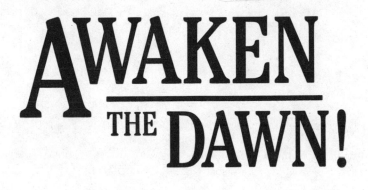

# AWAKEN THE DAWN!

## DISCOVERING THE JOY AND POWER OF EARLY MORNING PRAYER

# AWAKEN
## THE DAWN!

**DISCOVERING THE JOY AND POWER
OF EARLY MORNING PRAYER**

**ERNEST B. GENTILE**

AVAILABLE FROM:

BIBLE TEMPLE PUBLISHING
7545 NE GLISAN STREET
PORTLAND, OREGON 97213
1-800-777-6057


ISBN 0-914936-82-4


PRINTED IN U.S.A.

Dedicated to My Mother
**ICY OTIE GENTILE**
Who for over Half a Century Has Prayed
Unremittingly for Her Two Sons and Their Families

# TABLE OF CONTENTS

# Introduction
# My Adventure In
# Prayer

I received a most unusual gift for Christmas in 1982. Janice, my third daughter, gave me what appeared to be an ordinary book. My children know how I like books, so the feel and the shape of the wrapped package made it a very predictable item. To my surprise, however, upon opening the book I discovered the pages were all blank! "Hey, Dad," she said, "you're an author, so write your own book!"

About that time I was already quite serious about my personal prayer life. Early morning prayer for an hour each day in the living room was having an amazing effect on me. One morning, January 7th, 1983, I felt prompted to go for the blank book and start writing some thoughts about prayer. For the next few weeks my early morning rendezvous with the Lord became a blessed time of learning the "secrets" of prayer. With trembling hands I hastily wrote down the wonderful thoughts pouring into my mind as I prayed. An excitement in prayer gripped me that I had never known before. Then it dawned on me: my supposedly new "secrets" were actually concepts that appeared in the many prayer books on my shelf! The gold was there all of the time; I had just discovered it! The reader of prayer books was now ... praying.

As soon as I became consistent in morning prayer (I'm afraid it took several years!), it seemed only right to introduce the whole concept to our local church. Well, that too has taken several years, but we now have an early morning prayer service from 6 to 7, Monday through Friday, in our church sanctuary, and the people who are trying it, like it. Others are finding the same delight in their prayer times at home. Now, wonder of wonders, there are others in our church that are just as blessed about the merits of early morning prayer as I am!

We all want to upgrade our prayer lives, that is why we read books about prayer. Most people, though, need help to get started in a systematic program that they can maintain. In some ways it is like the dieting problem or flossing our teeth-- we know that we must do something, but how? Is there some way for me to get on a consistent program that will really work?

Let me be honest. I want to persuade you to adopt early morning prayer as a continuous, regular part of your life style. Why? Because this type of praying (I know from experience) will bless and enlarge your life and fill you with the wonderful joy of His presence. I believe that God's will for your life will unfold more freely for you through this method than any other approach. If you want to be a more consistent person of prayer, what is said through this book will be of great help to you. Early morning prayer really works, and thousands of people throughout the land will shout their confirmation if asked.

I contend that prayer, particularly early morning prayer, shaped the life, teachings, and ministry of Jesus. The wonderful "greatest story ever told" resulted from a life of prayer and communion with the heavenly Father. Let me talk to you about Jesus and His life and teaching of prayer in a very plain, non-theological, non-threatening way. I want you to be so inspired by these thoughts about Jesus and prayer that you too will rise to greet the Lord at daybreak--and discover the joy of continuous communion with our heavenly Father which results from starting your day with Him. My friend, let us arise each day and "awaken the dawn!"

*Ernest B. Gentile*

CHAPTER

# Awaken the Dawn

## The Sleeping Giant

We raced through the darkness of the pre-dawn morning, breaking the speed limit on the deserted and unfamiliar road. After traveling so far, it would be a shame to miss what some had said would be the highlight of our trip--sunrise on the Grand Canyon! It was so tempting to sleep in that morning. We were quite tired, and it was extremely cold outside the motel. But, we remembered, everyone who has seen sunrise on the Canyon says it is a most spectacular sight that no one should miss.

So Joy (my good wife) and I got up, dressed, and then rushed to make it on time. We noticed a few other brave souls parked at various intervals along the Canyon rim. Considering all the publicity, it was a pretty grim and foreboding setting. Soon, however, the light began to break over the horizon. What a sight!

The rising sun wondrously colored the clouds and sky, but equally spectacular was the continuously changing landscape as shadows were cast and lost on the rugged mountainous terrain. We stood there, trying desperately to drink in all the awesome majesty of the unfolding panorama. Finally, the sun was up, and turning to each other we exclaimed: "It was worth it to get up so early!" It was as though we had watched the birth and creation of the earth.

Ancient eastern peoples must have felt the same way about the rising sun. They not only used the sun to symbolize deity in their writings, but they also built their temples facing the east. Moses' Tabernacle and Solomon's Temple both faced the rising sun, because to Israel the sun typified the glory of God. For most people, ancient and modern, the day starts when the sunlight breaks across the land dispelling the night.

That wonderful Grand Canyon sunrise got me out of bed, but the tables are turned these days. Today, for instance, I saw the beautiful golden orb rise majestically over the eastern foothills of San Jose, California. The day was not just starting for me, however, I was very wide awake. I was returning home from spending two wonderful hours of prayer in the church sanctuary. I no longer let the sun summon me to its rising, instead, like David in Psalms, I find the joy of waking up the sun!

### David's Secret

David twice exclaims: "I will awaken the dawn![1] We must remember that David lived approximately one thousand

---

[1]    Psalms 57:8; 108:2. The Kings James Version says: "I myself will awake early." It does seem more accurate to use awake or awaken as with the NAS,NIV, RSV, NKJ,Rotherham, and the Interlinear Bible.

years before Christ. People did not understand the universe as we do today. They, of course, did not think of the earth rotating around the sun while it simultaneously revolved on its own axis. Their day began when the sun rose, ended when the sun set. They were a simple people whose lives revolved around a day of work during sunlight, and a night of rest while the sun was absent.

David makes a poetic expression out of a natural phenomenon. The new day is pictured as a sleeping person, and David declares that this day must be awakened by his praise and prayer so that it will come alive and provide him with fresh opportunities to serve the living God. F. Delitzsch comments:

> ...with the music of stringed instruments and with song he will awake the not yet risen dawn, the sun still slumbering in its chamber.[2]

David feels that he is to be a spiritual rooster, a harbinger of the sunrise, a herald that declares that God's day will be filled with God's blessings. Others may be awakened by the dawn, but David will awaken the dawn! David, unlike the heathen contemporaries of his day, does not worship the sun or its dawning, but he instead addresses himself directly to the great Creator-God who made and controls all things.

The day and all its potential comes from the hand of his God. Therefore, David as God's man, will rise before the sun and bring this sleeping giant of opportunities under the name of the Lord. He will order his day by seeking and praising his God before sunup. As David submits himself to God, the day presents itself as a servant to be commanded by the man of God. This pre-dawn prayer and praise so exhilarates him that

---

[2]   C.F. Keil and F. Delitzsch, *Commentary on the Old Testament*(Grand Rapids: Eerdmans, reprinted 1978), Vol. V, p. 178.

after he awakens the day he turns prophetically to the nations
and summons their participation in the worship of the
Almighty:

> I will give thanks to Thee, O Lord, among the
> peoples; I will sing praises to Thee among the
> nations.[3]

## Is there a Best Time to Pray?

Both the Bible and common sense dictate that a person
can pray anywhere at any time,[4] but the Bible does seem to
indicate that early morning prayer is most important and
possibly sets the course for prayer through the rest of the day.
Jesus certainly utilized the early morning hours for
prayer:

> And in the early morning, while it was still dark,
> He arose and went out and departed to a lonely
> place, and was praying there.[5]

The Book of Psalms is the one book of the Bible that
specializes in worship and prayer, so it is significant that
Psalms present a strong case for early morning prayer. Jesus
must have loved the Psalms for they were frequently on his
lips, even while He died on the cross. We can rightly assume
that these inspired words from Psalms had a strong influence
on the Son of Man as He sought communion with the
heavenly Father.

---

[3] Psalm 57:9.

[4] Note Ephesians 6:18.

[5] Mark 1:35.

5:3--    In the morning, O LORD, Thou wilt hear my voice;

         In the morning I will order my prayer to Thee and eagerly watch.

30:5--   For His anger is but
         for a moment,

         His favor is for a lifetime;

         Weeping my last for the night,
         But a shout of joy comes in the morning.

46:5--   God is in the midst of
         her, she will not be
         moved;

         God will help her when morning dawns.

55:17--  Evening and morning and at noon, I will complain and murmur,

         And he will hear my voice.

57:8--   Awake, my glory,
         Awake, harp and lyre,
         I will awaken the dawn!

59:16--  But as for me, I shall sing of Thy strength; Yes, I shall joyfully sing of Thy lovingkindness in the morning.

         For Thou has been my stronghold,
         And a refuge in the day of my distress.

63:1-- O God, thou art my God; early will I seek Thee:[6] my soul thirsteth for Thee, my flesh longeth for Thee in a dry and thirsty land, where no water is.[7]

88:13-- But I, O LORD, have cried out to Thee for help, and **in the morning** my prayer comes before Thee.

90:14-- O satisfy us **in the morning** with Thy Lovingkindness,

That we may sing for joy and be glad all our days.

---

[6] Charles H. Spurgeon comments on this verse that "The word 'early' has not only the sense of early in the morning, but that of eagerness, immediateness." He also says, "When the bed is the softest we are most tempted to rise at lazy hours; but when comfort is gone, and the couch is hard, if we rise the earlier to seek the Lord, we have much for which to thank the wilderness." From *The Treasury of David* (Byron Center, Michigan.: Associated Publishers & Authors, 1970),Vol.1, p.133.

[7] Psalm 63:1, King James Version.

92:1,2--    It is good to give thanks to the LORD,
And to sing praises to Thy name, O Most
High; To declare Thy lovingkindness **in
the morning,** And Thy faithfulness by
night.

108:2--    Awake, harp and lyre;
I will **awaken the
dawn!**

119:147--    I rise **before dawn** and cry for help;
I wait for Thy words.

143:8--    Let me hear Thy lovingkindness **in the**
morning; For I trust in Thee;
Teach me thy way in which I should walk;
For to Thee I lift up my soul.

I must warn you about these Scriptures....they get into
your very bones and cause you to do unusual things! While
other folks are still in bed or just getting up, you might find
yourself out on the church parking lot in the dim twilight
audibly praising the Lord, or praying fervently and quitely in
your living room before the rest of the family awakens. I find
myself chuckling about the new day as I look at the eastern
foothills and literally tell the sun to "get up, it is time for
God's kingdom to find expression and His will to be done.
Dawn, wake up!"

## Morning Prayer Around the World

It is exciting to conjecture what could happen if early morning prayer in every time zone could be initiated worldwide. This global concept has inspired me for a number of years, and it could be a very practical way that God would use in sheathing the Planet Earth in an envelope of prayer.

Think for a moment of the glorious possibilities! If Christians around the world would adopt early morning prayer (starting around 6 a.m. or just before sunrise), it means that as the earth rotates to meet the sun, there will be people in each time zone continuously starting their day with prayer as the "sun rises." Hopefully those same people will remain prayerful throughout their day. As the natural sun rises over the earth, the Lord Himself will be like the "Sun of righteousness"[8] pouring down His presence on His praying saints.

In a sense, then, the Church of Jesus Christ becomes "a house of prayer for (involving) all nations,[9] and Malachi 1:11 finds wonderful fulfillment:

"For from the rising of the sun, even to its setting, My name will be great among the nations, and in every place incense is going to be offered to My name, and a grain offering that is pure; for My name will be great among the nations," says the LORD of hosts.

---

8    Malachi 4:2, King James Version.

9    Isaiah 56:7; Mark 11:17.

## Command the Morning!

Another way of saying "Awaken the dawn!" would be "Command the morning!" Learn the marvelous secret of beginning each day with the certainty that "this is the day which the LORD has made; let us rejoice and be glad in it."[10] Today I am an instrument of God for the building of His kingdom!   Purge   your   mind   of   yesterday's disappointments. Do not allow disagreeable thoughts to gather like dark clouds shutting out the light of your dawn.

Start your day in the presence of the Lord, putting your trust unequivocally in Him.  Begin your day with prayer, and the negative, discouraging hangovers from yesterday will give way to shouts of anticipation!  The dawn brings you a new day, a fresh page for you life. As you begin your day, anchor your mind first on God and His Word, and then command your day--awaken your dawn-- by the confidence that is now released within you.

---

[10]   Psalm 118:24.

CHAPTER

# First Things First

## Start Your Day Right

Here are four good reasons why starting each day with prayer is the right way to start your day.

(1) *God is given first place.* It seems so logical to give God the first hour of each day. We Christians have been blessed by giving God the first day of the week and the first tenth (tithe) of our income, why not add the first hour of our day? Presenting God with the first hour is a tangible expression of trust and dependence.

In this deliberate, calculated action you make God number one in your life--you knowingly place yourself directly under His rule at the beginning of every day. This is truly a wise move, because God alone knows what is best for you, and He knows exactly how to bring it to pass. God is actually jealous to work and manipulate your life situations so that He will be glorified and you, His child, will be blessed.

I daily marvel at the divine provision for my day when I give Him the first hour: an impressive efficiency comes to my schedule. Even the unplanned interruptions cause me good and glorify the Father![1] A person that regularly starts the day with prayer will do more for God accidentally than he/she ever did on purpose!

Since I am a busy person while being remarkably poor in administration, I appreciate and depend on the "spiritual flow" that comes to a prayerful life. The other day, for instance, having presented to God the complexity of situations which I faced in the church and our academy, God proceeded to expedite solutions and maneuver people about throughout the day. Without making specific appointments, I "bumped into" people in just the right way to say the right things that needed to be said without bringing offense. Don't misunderstand me, I do make appointments, but sometimes God can arrange a simple divine encounter that is much more productive than a carefully orchestrated office appointment. People and things are moved along to proper placement when bound to that outcome through prayer. Consider this advice of Oswald Chambers:

> Get into the habit of dealing with God about everything. Unless in the first waking moment of the day you learn to fling the door wide back and let God in, you will work on a wrong level all day; but swing the door wide open and pray to your Father in secret, and every public thing will be stamped with the presence of God.[2]

---

[1]   I suggest that our morning prayer include asking God for provision in the unscheduled, unexpected interruptions that are bound to happen.

[2]   Oswald Chambers, *My Utmost for His Highest* (New York: Dodd, Mead & Co., Inc., 1935), p. 236.

After starting to tithe I soon discovered that more is accomplished with nine-tenths of an income and God's blessing than ever happened with all of an income without His blessing! Taking time for prayer has had the very same effect on my day, and caused me to adopt the following principle: I will get better mileage for my day if I will start with prayer.

Some people find it more advantageous to pray at some other time of day, and this is certainly commendable.I discussed this with our church elders (husbands and wives), and found that not everyone experienced the morning to be as easy and profitable for prayer as I have. One thing is for certain: for a consistent prayer life, a conscientious and efficient management of time will be required, and finding any time at all for prayer will be a matter for setting priorities.

Actually, we all have the right amount of time to do what God wants us to do, and we all have the same amount of time in a twenty-four hour day. "One's use and management of time depends upon one's system of values." says Paul Billheimer. "Whatever one deems of greatest importance will have priority." [3] I am simply saying that if a person truly wants to put first things first, why not consider making prayer that *literal* first thing on the agenda? This approach has worked wonders for me!

(2) *Prayer will be more dynamic.* Start your day with your mind on God. What a beginning! Come before Him open and expectant. Appear before the Lord as a servant before his master--fresh, eager, and ambitious to do what is bidden.

I know what you are thinking! My description is not exactly typical of the average person getting up in the morning. I do know that feeling. I thought that I was going to kill myself missing so much sleep! Then it "dawned" on me: go to bed earlier; adjust your television habits; exercise

---

[3]    Paul E. Billheimer, *Destined for the Throne* (Ft. Washington, Pennsylvania: Christian Literature Crusade, 1975), p. 132.

properly; come to grips with personal priorities.

Some studies indicate that when a person sits down to watch television a chemical reaction takes place in the body that affects the person in an addictive way. I know that I have found myself watching television for three hours at a stretch, and yet under the same circumstances I would fall asleep reading a book. Why do we feel so compelled to watch the 11 o'clock news when we have already watched the 10 o'clock news? The addiction can really get out of hand with one of those hand-held channel-changers! If you add cable television to the regular channels, you can find yourself watching two movies, the news, and scanning a dozen other channels--all at the same time!

To my amazement I found my whole life situation adjusting to the priority of prayer, rather than prayer adjusting to my life situation. This may be an exaggeration, but I think morning prayer is the one thing that can cure improper evening television habits and pull our frazzled lives back into order. The addictive fascinations of our worldly system will give way before the greater magnetism of the spiritual life. This, I maintain, is best accomplished for many of us through regular, early morning prayer.

Hopefully, then, sufficient sleep will be had during the previous hours so that you will be alert. When your mind and strength is at its best, give that time for your communion with God. Why should He be given your tired time or the left-overs? Give God the first hour of your day for prayer, and your prayer life will become dynamic! Many people have told me that their best intentions to pray were not realized because of life pressures until they started their day with prayer. Those same people testify that their prayer life then took on a dynamic it never had before.

I asked our academy sixth grade teacher the other day, "Don't you ever get tired of coming down to the early morning prayer meeting?" I realized that the woman was married, had older children at home, and was a grandmother. Surely she was stretching herself too much. "Oh, no," she said brightly, "I have so many things to pray about that I just wouldn't make it if I didn't take the time to pray!" A local pastor started early morning prayer after hearing me speak on the subject. "Tell me," I said, "has it made a difference in your life?" He broke into a grand smile and said, "Things are just going wonderful, and I now find that I have to pray more than an hour--there are so many prayer requests!" I appreciate and confirm the testimony of Bill Hybels in his excellent book, *Too Busy Not to Pray:*

> My life with God is a constant adventure, and it all begins with prayer. Regular prayer, early in the morning, alone with Him. Prayer that listens as well as speaks.[4]

(3) *Prayer becomes continuous.* How in the world does a person "pray without ceasing"?[5] Continuous prayer is a staggering concept, but if you can begin your day with an hour of serious, Spirit-quickened prayer, you will find yourself clothed throughout the day with an aura or atmosphere of prayer that will amaze you. Paul did not mean that we are to pray continuously over prayer lists and problems, but he did mean that Christians can live in an attitude of prayer and communion with God even when secular tasks are being performed. When this process of early morning prayer is repeated every day, the life of prayer more and more becomes continuous and possible through the Holy Spirit. Set the tone of the day with early morning prayer, and spirituality then tends to prevail and prayer becomes easier.

(4) *Hindrances are eliminated.* It appears that most

---

4    Bill Hybels, *Too Busy Not to Pray* (Downers Grove: InterVarsity Press, 1988), p.151.

5    1 Thessalonians 5:17.

Christians and their church leaders have one frustration in common: inconsistency in prayer, and this embarrassing trait is fed by four basic root problems:

Time pressure
Administrative jumble
Weakness of the flesh
Lack of fresh content

These four reasons are the most frequently given by ministers,[6] but I hear homemakers saying the same thing, "Pray for me; I am so busy and so tired I can't seem to pray much."

### Eliminate the Four Hindrances!

For me a consistent early morning prayer schedule provides the answer to all four of these hindrances; allow me to explain.

*Time pressure.* Even if there is a busy schedule, the most important thing is always done first--you pray. And, if there are other things demanding time, some other less important thing will have to be dropped--not prayer! Like many busy people, I use the Day-Timer for my daily scheduling. The publishers advocate that you write out the things which must be done during your day, then, number the events in the order of their importance. If a person works on the most important thing first, he/she will feel fulfilled at the end of the day knowing that even if everything was not done, at least the

---

6    Terry Muck, *Liberating the Leader's Prayer Life*, The Leadership Library, Vol. 2 (Waco: Word Books, 1985), p. 154ff. An excellent book that deals with the problems of prayerlessness and shares how various leaders have solved this problem in their own lives.

most important things were done. I used to go day after day, confused and ashamed that I could not mark down that prayer was being offered to God. That has changed. Join me in writing "prayer" in front of all other priorities and appointments, and let's do it!

Andrew Murray wrote a classic on *The Prayer Life*. He describes "the sin of prayerlessness," and he advises:

> The greatest stumbling-block in the way of victory over prayerlessness is the secret feeling that we shall never obtain the blessing of being delivered from it.[7]

I humbly suggest that each of us is capable of deliverance by simply wrestling the control of our time out of the tyranny of time pressure. This can be done by making the commitment to consistently start each day with prayer.

*Administrative jumble.* Even if there is a confusing, unpredictable schedule to face, starting with prayer in an uninterrupted time will settle your mind and enable God to release His blessing upon all that your day brings. Let me share another quote from Murray:

---

7    Andrew Murray, *The Prayer Life* (Grand Rapids: Zondervan, new edition 1988), p. 15. Read his first three chapters for some challenging thoughts about the deeper implications of "The Sin and Cause of Prayerlessness," "The Fight Against Prayerlessness," and "How To Be Delivered from Prayerlessness."

If I commit myself for the day to the Lord Jesus, then I may rest assured that it is His eternal almighty power which has taken me under its protection and which will accomplish everything for me.[8]

The day is not really yours.You are merely a steward of that which belongs to Another; however, when you the servant are under His authority, you may command the day to your godly wishes. Sometimes in these early morning hours new ideas, concepts approaches are born in your mind. You will come to rely on these wonderful insights as you perceive that the Master is indeed overseeing your day. Sometimes this oversight will be silent, and at other times your mind will receive such clear, clean direction that you cannot help but know that it is the Lord of your life who is helping you. As an example, the other day I brought to the Lord my desire to see more children involved in our pre-service prayer meeting before Sunday School. Suddenly, I saw a mental picture of the children surrounding various teachers in our Prayer Room. We have now successfully implemented this procedure that I had simply overlooked before.

I have discovered that people that I have tried futilely to contact by natural means, suddenly come across my path and in just a few moments I am able to do more in the unexpected contact than if I had been able to schedule an appointment. By administering your life through prayer, you allow the Holy Spirit special freedom to work the miraculous for you. It is an exciting way to live!

*Weakness of the flesh.* Even if your flesh and dedication is weak (we're all in the same boat on this one!), a set discipline of morning prayer will do much to help you conquer

---

[8]    Murray, p. 21.

your weakness. Routine does not necessarily destroy spirituality and spontaneity, rather it serves as the vehicle for the working of the Holy Spirit.

Jesus Himself recognized the weakness of the flesh. The next time you contemplate praying for an hour, it might be well to remember His words in Gethsemane:

> So, you men could not keep watch with Me for an hour? Keep watching and praying, that you may not enter into temptation; the spirit is willing but the flesh is weak.[9]

*Lack of fresh content.* When the ministers in the survey listed the fourth hindrance to consistency in prayer as "lack of fresh content," they were not saying that there is a lack of *things* to pray for. Rather, they were saying that there was a lack of inspiration, incentive, concern, faith--and, probably most importantly, a sense of God's involvement with their own concerns.

To pray daily in the same way for the same things is indeed spiritually debilitating. Monotonous, wooden prayer ritual easily overwhelms inspiring devotional prayer.

A number of times I have actually gone to sleep on my knees, only to wake with a deeper shame that my prayer life was so anemic. Two things have helped me overcome this. First, I set a time, I put prayer on my schedule. Then, I must also stir myself to pray during that time. I change my posture: stand, sit, walk, lie down, kneel. I pray out loud in English. I pray silently. At times I pray in the Spirit-given prayer language of glossolalia or "tongues."[10] Even if it seems your

---

9    Matthew 26:40, 41.

10   Note 1 Corinthians 14 where tongues is particularly described as a gift to enable our personal communication with God.

prayer life is dying, start praying with diligence and fervor each morning on a regular basis, and you will soon discover a new freshness and inspiration taking place. You will be surprised at the stimulating prayer-thoughts that the Holy Spirit will bring to you if you will take the time to listen! Do not be discouraged by dryness or low feelings.

One of the most effective ways to involve your total person in prayer is to use the Bible. Learn to pray the words of the Bible, personalizing the verses as your pray-read. Pump enthusiasm into your daily morning prayer, and you will find prayer will produce a fresh, new, and vigorous spiritual life. Combine enthusiasm with proper time management and you will have a winner! Apply this golden verse:

But **seek first** His kingdom and His righteousness; and all these things shall be added to you.[11]

---

[11] Matthew 6:33.

C H A P T E R

# Relationship Takes a Chunk of Time

## What? A Whole Hour!

Why start the day with *an hour* of prayer?

(1) *Give God a good chunk.* To begin each day with an hour of prayer is that commitment that will make the difference. Most of us are trying to fit God into our lives--five minutes here, ten minutes there. Instead, each of us should fit our lives around God, and this is done through consignment of time. A wise man once gave this piece of advice on starting your day in such a way:

> The idea is to take a chunk of time big enough to mean something to you--and then, give that chunk to God.[1]

---

1    Barbara Bartocci, "One Hour That Can Change Your Life," Readers Digest, March 1984, p. 14.

An hour is a substantial, reasonable gift of your time to present to God every day. This idea is catching on world-wide, and an increasing number of church leaders are advocating daily one-hour prayer. C. Peter Wagner, well-known church growth specialist, makes this comment:

> Since prayer is essentially a relationship with the Father, it takes time--minutes on the clock. Most of us have come to realize that this is true of our relationship to our spouses. It is also true of our relationship to our Heavenly Father.

> If time for prayer is important, how much is needed? I find myself agreeing with Larry Lea that one hour a day is a realistic goal for most Christians in general, including leaders.[2]

We moderns look for justification in giving up such an important block of time. Our results-oriented society has programmed our thinking so heavily that we even evaluate prayer in terms of whether or not it is a practical tool for our own benefit. The fruitfulness of prayer and the personal value of prayer are not easily measured or understood by such superficial analysis. Those who have practiced starting their days with an hour of prayer have found more than commercial benefit, they have found the joy of His presence. Such people talk of having their empty lives now filled with God's presence, finding peace of mind and quietness of soul, seeing the things of life in proper perspective, and finding God in every circumstance.

Dick Eastman has written a whole book on taking an hour per day for prayer. In his opening "challenge" on the

---

2    C. Peter Wagner, "Praying for Leaders," *World Evangelization* (Vol. 15, No. 53, July-Aug. 1988), p. 24.

subject he states clearly the accumulated power of consistently applying this principle:

> And think of the impact this daily gift of sixty minutes will have on a troubled world. One hour each day for an entire year equals 365 hours, or forty-five continuous "eight-hour" days. Imagine asking your employer for six weeks off work next year so you can spend the time with Jesus praying for the world. That's the power of giving God just sixty minutes a day (when projected for a full year).[3]

(2) *Take time to get started.* Break loose from that "fast-food" mentality that wants prayer answers served up like hamburgers within two minutes! It actually take more than a few minutes to get adjusted for serious prayer and to "get into" prayer. When I know that I will be praying for an hour, I settle down with earnest intent to pray; my mind settles into a spiritual frame of reference; the secular transitions to the spiritual. You may change TV channels by simply clicking a button, but most of us need a little longer to open our minds to the spiritual realm.

By blocking out this choice period of the day and making it long enough to pray effectively, the total person (spirit, soul, and body) can adjust and participate. One hour daily will indeed bless and improve your life. A personal revolution will be launched!

(3) *Heed the challenge of Jesus.* Once in the Garden of Gethsemane, Jesus plead with his followers to pray with Him for an hour.[4] I take this as a timeless invitation to all His

---

3    Dick Eastman, *The Hour That Changes the World* (Grand Rapids: Baker Book House, 1978), p. 9.

4    Matthew 26:40, 41; Mark 14:37.

people; after all, we are dealing with a timeless principle, so why should we not claim it?

(4) *Listen to the experts.* Those who have developed the daily habit of praying for an hour or more are the greatest advocates of this exercise; such people, of course, should be our mentors, not those who have never tried serious prayer. There is in fact an addiction to prayer that attends this morning habit. Once you experience it, you wonder how you ever survived without it! David Brainerd, the famous prayer warrior, exclaimed: "Oh! One hour with God infinitely exceeds all the pleasure and delights of this lower world."

It is not uncommon for those who have become accustomed to praying an hour to testify that they now want to pray more than an hour! I am delighted that several of my pastoral friends in the city where I live have started praying with this same approach.

There are presently thousands of people participating in daily hour-long sessions of prayer both at home and abroad. Most of these people are using some simple system such as Larry Lea's format of the Lord's Prayer,[5] Dick Eastman's sixty-minute pace system,[6] or Glenn Sheppard's Global Prayer Strategy that advocates early morning prayer for different

---

[5] Pastor Larry Lea is now attempting to recruit 300,000 people across the country to commit to one hour per day for prayer. See his book, *Could You Not Tarry One Hour?* (Rockwall, Texas: Church on the Rock, 1984).

[6] Thousands of Christians have been committed to daily prayer through Eastman's *Change the World School of Prayer.* See his book, already mentioned, *The Hour that Changes the World.*

sections of the world each day.[7] Having some structure to your approach is very helpful; it keeps you consistent and persistent. I have found great delight in a variety of approaches, including the use of a prayer map to pray for the nations of the world.[8] More will be said later about the how and format of prayer.

Perhaps the greatest examples of praying Christians and churches today are to be found in Korea. Prayer is practiced, not discussed. C. Peter Wagner shares this observation:

> I think my deepest impression of Korea was the extraordinary pervasive sense of prayer I found in all the churches. Every church has a dawn prayer meeting at 4:30 or 5:00a.m. every single day. It is so important that the senior pastor of most multiple-staff churches visits or leads that meeting every morning. When I asked why, several said simply, "That's where the power comes from." Most churches have an all-night prayer meeting on Friday nights that the pastor often attends.[9]

One of the greatest advocates of morning prayer is Paul Y. Cho, pastor of the world's largest church in Seoul, Korea. His books and ministry pulsate with a powerful conviction

---

7   Global Prayer Strategy Manual, PO Box 888-850, Atlanta, Georgia 30356, USA.

8   I think the best map is the one produced by Jack McAlister, *World Prayer 2000*, Box 922020, Sylmar, California 91392.

9   C. Peter Wagner, "The Korean Experience," *World Evangelization Bulletin*, No. 24 (September 1981), p. 6.

about the effectiveness of prayer. He cautions that, "In learning to pray, we must not be in a hurry." He goes on to say that "getting up early every morning helps me to have the time necessary to pray."[10]


### Sweet Hour of Prayer

The words to "Sweet Hour of Prayer," one of the world's most popular prayer hymns, was written by a man who could not see. In 1842 the Reverend William W. Walford, a blind English clergyman, dictated this inspirational poem of prayer. His physical impairment seems to have been a blessing in disguise, for his words reveal a heart for God and a special illumination of the power of prayer.

Truthfully, this hymn has bothered me for years. As a teenager, I played the piano for Sunday School and church services, and this hymn was frequently requested for congregational singing. Sitting at the bench, I wondered what it would be like to pray for an hour on a daily basis. Now, thank God, I know what Reverend Walford meant, and that great hymn is a living reality in my heart. Please take a moment to read and interact with these well-known words, and then I will share with you in the next chapter why I think Jesus particularly used the early morning time for prayer.

Sweet hour of prayer, sweet hour of prayer,
    That calls me from a world of care,
And bids me at my Father's throne
    Make all my wants and wishes known;

In seasons of distress and grief,
    My soul has often found relief,

---

[10] See his practical suggestions in *Prayer: Key to Revival* (Waco, Texas: Word Books, 1984).

And oft escaped the tempter's snare,
    By thy return, sweet hour of prayer.

Sweet hour of prayer, sweet hour of prayer,
    Thy wings shall my petition bear,
To Him whose truth and faithfulness
    Engage the waiting soul to bless;
And since He bids me seek His face,
    Believe His word and trust His grace,
I'll cast on Him my every care,
    And wait for thee, sweet hour of prayer.

Sweet hour of prayer, sweet hour of prayer,
    May I thy consolation share.
Till, from Mount Pisgah's lofty height,
    I view my home, and take my flight:
This robe of flesh I'll drop, and rise
    To seize the everlasting prize;
And shout, while passing thro' the air,
    Farewell, farewell, sweet hour of prayer.

CHAPTER

# Discovery of an Amazing Treasure

## Finding the Third Servant Song

One of my most exciting Bible discoveries happened during an early morning prayer service in the church sanctuary. On this particular morning people were each having private, individual prayer in various parts of the auditorium, and I was walking slowly along the front of the sanctuary, praying in a personalized way some words from the Book of Isaiah.

My eyes fell upon Isaiah 50:4,5. As I read the following words, it was as though light broke in upon my mind. I suddenly realized that I had come upon both an amazing confirmation of early morning prayer--and perhaps the very foundation of Jesus' prayer ministry.

The Lord GOD has given Me the tongue of
disciples,
That I may know how to sustain the weary one with a
word.
He awakens Me morning by morning,
He awakens My ear to listen as a disciple.
The Lord GOD has opened my ear;
And I was not disobedient,
Nor did I turn back.

*The Natural question:* "Who is this person that the
LORD awakens each morning and trains as His own disciple?"
*The simple answer:* "This is the predicted Messiah
(Christ) that will come as a special Servant of the LORD to
redeem God's people."
This passage from Isaiah is one of four beautiful passages
in Isaiah that are called "The Servant Songs" because Christ
the Servant is introduced by the Lord, or speaks in His own
person, or is described by others. All four of these Servant
Songs breathe the same sentiments and certainly express the
mind and mission of Jesus Christ, the Servant of the Songs.[1]
Isaiah chapter 50 is the foundation for my believing so
strongly in early morning prayer. It now seems so apparent to
me that the secret of Jesus' successful ministry can be traced
to His dynamic prayer encounters with His heavenly Father at
the beginning of each day. I suggest that we too can have this
same Servant Song dynamically real in our lives. This will

---

[1] The four songs are Isaiah 42:1-4 (with verses 5-9 as a
connecting link with what follows); 49:1-6 (with verses
7-13 as a connecting link); 50:4-9 (possibly with verses
10, 11 as a connecting link); and 52:10-53:12. For an
interesting discussion of the Songs see F.F. Bruce,
*New Testament Development of Old Testament
Themes* (Grand Rapids: Eerdmans, 1968), Chapter
VII.

become apparent as we examine more closely the meaning of four distinct phases of the third Song.

## "The Tongue of Disciples"

When Isaiah states that: "The Lord GOD has given Me the tongue of disciples," he is prophetically stating that God has given the Christ "words of wisdom" (Living Bible) or "an instructed tongue" (New International Version), or as the Good News Bible words it: "The Sovereign LORD has taught me what to say..." Edward J. Young helpfully explains the expression like this:

> The phrase designates a tongue such as learned or skilled men have, and hence a ready, expert tongue. The learned are instructed by the Lord; the tongue belongs to one taught of God, and so it is the tongue of a person instructed and illumined by His Spirit.[2]

Jesus certainly used this wise skill in bringing hope to discouraged people. In His home town of Nazareth, "all were speaking well of Him, and wondering at the gracious words which were falling from His lips."[3] When He concluded His Sermon on the Mount, "the multitudes were amazed at His teaching."[4] On one occasion the temple guard, who had been sent to arrest Jesus, returned awestruck and empty handed. When the chief priests and Pharisees demanded, "Why did you

---

[2] Edward J. Young, *The Book of Isaiah* (Grand Rapids: Eerdmans, 1972), Vol. III, p. 298.

[3] Luke 4:22.

[4] Matthew 7:28.

not bring Him?" they could only answer, "Never did a man speak the way this man speaks." [5]

Jesus made no secret of His divine help; freely He admitted, "My teaching is not Mine, but His who sent Me." [6] I like the beautiful passage in Psalm 45:2, which describes the effect accomplished in Jesus because He awakened each morning to learn of the Father:

> Thou art fairer than the sons of men;
> Grace is poured upon Thy lips;
> Therefore God has blessed Thee forever.

Jesus, without any formal rabbinical training, became the most excellent teacher and encourager of His day. It is true that everyone did not accept all He said, but no one would challenge that He spoke with compelling power and conviction. The people from His part of the country asked incredulously, while admitting the dynamism of His message:

> "Where did this man get this wisdom, and these miraculous powers? Is not this the carpenter's son?...Where then did this man get all these things?" And they took offense at Him. [7]

What is that special something that a certain speaker has that rivets your attention, feeds your soul, and sends you forth boldly doing the will of God? In contrast the sermon can be sheer dullsville, the mind wanders, it even becomes a torturous experience to sit and listen. I have experienced it both ways, as a preacher and as a listener.

---

[5]   John 7:45, 46.

[6]   John 7:16.

[7]   Matthew 13:54-57.

My four children grew up listening to my sermons Sunday after Sunday. My poor wife has heard me preach thousands of messages. Joy and I are so proud of our children --and always have been--but sometimes those kids would be unmerciful! I suspect that I'm not too different from the average pastor going home from the morning service. Driving away from the church (discretely waiting at least a few blocks), I would casually ask what they thought of the sermon. It astounded me how instantly and articulately they would analyze my masterpiece. The *coup de maitre* came from my teenaged son more than a decade ago: "Dad," he said, "if you would just tell us *first* what you're going to say, we would know what you're talking about!"

It is hard to preach a good sermon, and we preachers are the biggest critics of other people's sermons. Sometimes I go to a convention where big-name speakers are waxing eloquent, and my wife has to keep nudging me to keep me awake! The ultimate, though, is a man who used to visit our church every so often. The poor fellow was hard of hearing and so he wore a hearing aid. The apparatus served him well in church, however, because he simply turned the aid off when he got tired of listening! He didn't fool me, though, because a certain glazed look came across his eyeballs.

My wife told me the other day (after listening to me for forty years) that I am now preaching the way she has always wished I would preach. My grown, married children are still in the church listening to me, and they are saying the same thing, so I guess things are better. What makes the difference? What have I changed? Is there some new approach?

I feel that two things are essential for a good message: find what God wants to say to a given audience, and say it in a relevant, understandable, enjoyable, enthusiastic way.

Morning prayer supplies me with both! One reason that I can write this chapter with such fervor is that I have experienced to a small degree what Jesus experienced as He fulfilled the Isaiah 50 Servant Song. It is in prayer that the message is birthed, and it is through prayer that heavenly unction enables one to bring with impact the flaming words of God.

No words more dreaded come to a pastor's ears than those given by a departing member of the flock: "I have decided to leave the church, pastor, because you no longer feed me."

The connection between early morning prayer and a ministry of hope and encouragement cannot be taken lightly. We must have something before we can give it, and this waiting on God does something profound in the minister. About one hundred years ago a man gave some significant studies on this very subject. Called by some "the prince of preachers," Charles Haddon Spurgeon filled his London Tabernacle with 6,000 people weekly. His advice to student preachers is recorded in *Lectures to My Students*. In Chapter III, "The Preacher's Private Prayer," one discovers the real reason for Spurgeon's dynamic ministry--prayer!

> All that a college course can do for a student is coarse and external compared with the spiritual and delicate refinement obtained by communion with God. Your prayers will be your ablest assistants while your discourses are yet upon the anvil. While other men, like Esau, are hunting for their portion, you, by the aid of prayer, will find the savory meat near at home, and may say in truth what Jacob said so falsely, "The Lord brought it to me."

> The closet is the best study. The commentators are good instructors, but the Author Himself is far better, and prayer makes a direct appeal to Him

and enlists Him in our cause.Let your fleece lie on
the threshing-floor of supplication till it is wet with
the dew of heaven. [8]

One of the most prolific and profound writers on prayer
dates from the Civil War days. The writings of Edward M.
Bounds still throb with what he and Spurgeon called "the
unction." This term refers to that wonderful presence of God
that is attendant with ministry that has waited before the
throne of God. Bounds stresses the importance of a prepared
heart that results from seasons of prayer, particularly early
morning prayer.

The men who have done the most for God in this
world have been early on their knees. He who
fritters away the early morning, its opportunity and
freshness, in other pursuits than seeking God's will
make poor headway seeking Him the rest of the
day. If God is not first in our thoughts and efforts
in the morning, He will be in the last place the
remainder of the day. [9]

### "He Awakens Me"

When and how does God give His wonderful education
to His Servant? The answer is disarmingly simple! God will
speak to His Son the first thing every morning when He
awakens. In fact God Himself will be involved to such an

---

[8]    Charles H. Spurgeon, *Lectures to My Students* (Grand
       Rapids: Baker Book House, reprinted 1977), pp. 40-
       52.

[9]    E.M. Bounds, *Power through Prayer* (Grand Rapids:
       Zondervan, 1974, fifteenth printing!), p. 42.

extent that Jesus can say, "He awakens Me morning by morning..."[10] Dare we appropriate such a wonderful promise for ourselves as well?

Jesus will understand that when He awakens each morning, it is not just the result of sleep patterns or biological rhythms. The time of awakening is actually a divine summons for God's Servant to present Himself before His Sovereign Lord. There is more intended, however, than the mere physical awakening! This is a summons to hear the Master's voice bringing instruction for the day. The summons clearly states, "He awakens My ear to listen as a disciple." The Father will gain the attention of His Servant so that He may instruct Him.

I was thrilled when this revelation first came to me. My immediate thought was that knowing this truth will certainly help me bound out of bed in the morning, brilliantly awake and sparklingly spiritual. Alas, I have not found this to be so. As the years have passed, it is no easier to get up and seek the Lord than it was before! It certainly is true that the experience of prayer is greater than ever, and the enjoyment of being with God is at an all-time high for me. Tremendous answers to prayer have resulted from seeking Him early. Why, then, doesn't God make it easier for me to get up? After all, if He awakens me, why doesn't He help get me up? The best answer I know is given by our friend Edward Bounds--but, I warn you, he doesn't hold back any punches!

> A desire for God which cannot break the chains of sleep is a weak thing and will do but little good for God after it has indulged itself fully. The desire for God that keeps so far behind the devil and the world at the beginning of the day will never catch up.

---

[10]    Isaiah 50:4.

It is not simply the getting up that puts men to the front and makes them captain generals in God's hosts, but it is the ardent desire which stirs and breaks all self-indulgent chains. But the getting up gives vent, increases, and strength to the desire. If they had lain in bed and indulged themselves, the desire would have been quenched. The desire aroused them and put them on the stretch for God, and this heeding and acting on the call gave their faith its grasp on God and gave to their hearts the sweetest and fullest revelation of God, and this strength of faith and fullness of revelation made them saints by eminence, and the halo of their sainthood has come down to us. [11]

May the Lord help us to be like Jesus, of whom it was said: "in the early morning, while it was still dark, He arose and went out and departed to a lonely place, and was praying there."[12] The Son of God habitually, regularly, early in the morning, sought the face of God; Jesus refused the chains of self-indulgence, thereby becoming the first of many who claim the promises of the Servant Song.

## "God Has Opened My Ear"

It is one thing to be physically awakened out of sleep, but it is something particularly wonderful to have your inner, spiritual "ear" awakened by God to the truths of the Spirit. In Isaiah 50:5, the Servant of the Lord says, "The Lord GOD has opened My ear..." In a similar passage in Psalm 40:6, a text

---

[11]  Bounds, p. 43.

[12]  Mark 1:35.

that clearly refers to the Lord Jesus Christ,[13] the Servant says "My ears Thou hast opened."

He did *nothing* on His own initiative, but rather listened each day for the voice of instruction and/or the impressions of the Spirit which would enable Him to do the will of the Father. Consider His words:

> Jesus therefore answered and was saying to them, "Truly, truly, I say to you, the Son can do nothing of Himself, unless it is something He sees the Father doing; for whatever the Father does, these things the Son also does in like manner. For the Father loves the Son, and shows Him all things that He Himself is doing; and greater things than these will He show Him that you may marvel... I can do nothing on My own initiative. As I hear, I judge; and My judgement is just, because I do not seek My own will, but the will of Him who sent Me."[14]

During times of early morning and solitary prayer, Jesus received the heavenly manna with which to feed the multitudes. Undoubtedly the principles of the Sermon on the Mount resulted from the "ear-opening" experience of prayer. The Lord's Prayer was birthed and refined in the actual performance of prayer. By the revelation that came to Him through prayer, Jesus both understood His disciples and discerned the strategy of the devil.

Every public figure who seeks a following understands the importance of advertising and publicity. However Isaiah 42:2 declares that the Messiah "will not cry out or raise His

---

[13]   Quoted in Hebrews 10:5-9.

[14]   John 5:19, 20, 30; 8:28, 29, 38, 42; 9:4; 10:37.

voice, nor make His voice heard in the street..."[15] Jesus, in defiance of man's long-established method, "warned the people not to make Him known"--that is, He would not publicize Himself or run a popularity campaign; instead, He would wait daily for God's directives and be obedient to the Father's will. Prayer made this principle real to Him.

In the early days of my San Jose pastorate a prophecy was given to me that if I would be faithful in going out to minister to other churches the Lord would add people to our church. With my sales training--and my determination to knock on doors to reach people--I found this hard to believe. But, it has proven to be true. The enlarging of our church through my own exhausting efforts has proven rather fruitless, but invariably each year people are added to the church as I am obedient to go out to help others.[16]

The house in which we live is the result of prayer. I mention this because God is very concerned about our personal needs, and He will "open our ear" with insights of what to do if we will seek Him. By making prayer a daily regimen, we allow God abundant "lead in" time to do His will in our daily life situations, for His glory. Paul captured this concept when he said, "And we know that God causes all things to work together for good to those who love God..."[17] Joy and I had prayed for six months about moving, but not really doing anything about it. Then, suddenly, we both became acutely aware that the time had come. The Lord had "opened our ear" in the sense that we perceived what we were

---

[15] See the fulfillment in Matthew 12:18-21.

[16] I feel that we should endeavor in our churches to use the very best principles of the science of church growth, but with those methods must be coupled the unique guidance that comes through prayer.

[17] Romans 8:28.

to do. We immediately began looking, and quickly found our present house and sold our other house as well (shortly thereafter real estate prices began to escalate sharply!).

Paul clearly declares that the Spirit will bring wisdom and spiritual perception to us. Things are revealed to us "through the Spirit" and we are taught "by the Spirit." In other words we too have our "ears" or spiritual perception opened. [18] Surely prayer is the key facilitator of this process. The cry of the Spirit to the seven churches of Asia was "He who has an ear, let him hear what the Spirit says to the churches."[19] A praying church will know the will of God.

## "And I Was Not Disobedient"

The rest of the third Servant Song tells us what we already know: Jesus was obedient to the instruction of His Father, even though it meant public humiliation and physical torture. One translation says: "The Lord Jehovah opened for Me the ear, and I resisted not..."[20] Jesus was able to fulfil verse six of Isaiah 50, following through in doing God's will, because of the inner strength that came to Him daily in His times of personal, solitary prayer. How else could He continue in a ministry which He knew would kill Him?

> I gave My back to those who strike Me,
> And My cheeks to those who pluck out the beard;
> I did not cover My face from humiliation and spitting.
> For the Lord GOD helps Me,

---

[18] 1 Corinthians 2:10-16.

[19] Revelation 2:7, 11, 17, 29; 3:6, 13, 22.

[20] J. A. Alexander, *The Prophecies of Isaiah* (Grand Rapids: Zondervan, 1970 edition), p. 251.

Therefore, I am not disgraced...[21]


## Four Key Thoughts

Consider the wonderful impact the third Servant Song can make in our spiritual lives. If we will start our day early in the presence of the Lord, commune with Him, allow His impressions and directions to fill our minds, and then go forth to obey what we perceive God is saying to us--what results we will have!

Let us, therefore, as disciples of the Christ, personally apply the four key thoughts of the Song that the Master has so beautifully modeled for us:

1. *Awake Properly.* Consider that it is God Who awakens you each day, and respond as though summoned to the court of the great King.

2. *Listen Carefully.* Let Him awaken your spiritual ear to listen. You will come to understand His will and direction for your life. It is through prayer that a person is prepared to hear spiritual truths. Jesus would often punctuate His teachings by the cry, "He who has ears to hear, let him hear."[22] The Son of God wanted people to know the will of His Father, but He knew that this ability to hear resulted from communion with the Father.

3. *Obey Diligently.* Trust the impressions that are born

---

[21] Isaiah 50:6,7. Note the fulfillment in Matthew 26:67; 27:30; Mark 15:19; Luke 22:63.

[22] This expression occurs fifteen times in the New Testament, seven in the Gospels and eight in Revelation; as, Matthew 11:15; 13:9,43; Mark 4:9, 23; Luke 8:8; 14:35.

in times of prayer, and seek to be obedient to the convictions placed in your heart. Remember that if you ask God for bread, He will give you bread--not a stone![23] Realize that when you ask God for direction, He will seek to make that direction clear to you.

4. *Suffer Gracefully.* Even though, like Jesus, your ministry and destiny may be difficult and filled with suffering, endure patiently--don't turn back! Let the will and Word of God find fulfillment in your life.

### His Unbroken Fellowship

Jesus lived in an unbroken fellowship with the heavenly Father that was initiated by starting each day in the Father's presence. May we all learn that the way we begin the day will affect the rest of the day.

Jesus would certainly pray whenever special needs arose. Sometimes He prayed during the night while others slept. His prayer in Gethsemane is clearly an example of prayer for an important event. [24] He prayed whenever and wherever He could. He certainly was not limited to just morning prayer or one particular location. As Hebert Lockyer says:

Jesus, who had nowhere to lay His head, had no fixed inner-chamber during His public career. His was no prayer-closet to which He could retire to make easier and habitual His fellowship with God. He loved Nature and often His prayer-chambers were the deserts, mountains and solitary places which He sought for their freedom from the

---

23  Matthew 7:9-11.

24  Matthew 26:36-46; Mark 14:32-42; Luke 22:40-46.

discordant voices of earth. [25]

Jesus' way of prayer has powerfully impacted my life. The habit of prayer, this living in the spirit of prayer, has been best achieved for me by regularly starting the day with prayer. Morning prayer sets my mind and heart toward the Lord. Distractions and intrusions still come, problems still arise, but these things can no longer overwhelm and defeat me.

Some Christians feel that they must choose between the disciplined form of prayer and the haphazard way. [26] Others declare they wish to develop a prayer life style. Prayer certainly is so personal that each of us must find his/her own style and approach. It does seem, however, that starting the day with at least an hour of prayer admirably fulfills the necessity of discipline, while at the same time initiating a state of mind and spirit which encourages haphazard and emergency praying throughout the rest of the day. This approach, consistently applied, produces a sensible and inspiring life style of prayer. Spiritual resources never thought accessible become available. An awareness of God's Spirit begins to pervade our lives.

## The Delight of the Christ

The desire of the heart to seek the Lord will find reinforcement through discipline, and then out of that discipline will come delight. This daily regimen of consistently putting God first in the early hours of the day will bring the

---

[25] Herbert Lockyer, *All the Prayers of the Bible* (Grand Rapids: Zondervan, 1959), p. 188.

[26] Note the examples given by Terry Muck, *Liberating the Leader's Prayer Life* (Waco: Word Books, 1985), pp. 38-45.

person of prayer into an unbelievable delight. Jesus Himself "learned obedience from the things which He suffered." [27]

Through the years I have tended to think of Jesus as having total, independent spirituality and power from the beginning of His ministry. After researching His life of prayer, however, I must conclude that the Son of Man was very dependent on His heavenly Father's directions and blessings, and this obedience did indeed require discipline. His temptations and trials of the flesh were conquered through prayer and faith that issued from sincere desire, consistent discipline, and joyful delight. Because He Himself underwent the same struggles that we experience, He is now able to be a most sympathetic intercessor for us at the right hand of God the Father. The following verses show us a caring Christ who understands how hard the pressure may be, but also assures us of help.

> Therefore, He had to be made like ("to be like us, His brothers," Living Bible) His brethren in all things that He might become a merciful and faithful high priest in things pertaining to God, to make propitiation for the sins of the people. For since He Himself was tempted in that which He has suffered, He is able to come (immediately!) to the aid of those who are tempted. [28]

Many of us like to claim the provisions of Luke 11:9, 10, when we pray: "ask, and it shall be given to you; seek, and you shall find; knock, and it shall be opened to you." This translation, however, can be misleading. A superficial interpretation would take a person directly from desire to

---

27    Note that this expression is found in the context of prayer (Hebrews 5:7-9).

28    Hebrews 2:17, 18.

delight, simply receiving because one asks. But the text actually teaches a persistency and tenacity in prayer that comes only from disciplined living. The Williams Translation accurately captures this thought by making the verbs progressive: "...keep on asking...keep on seeking...keep on knocking..."[29] The finding and doing of God's will brings great delight.

> Then I said, "Behold, I come:
> In the scroll of the book it is written of me;
> I delight to do Thy will, O my God;
> Thy Law is within my heart."[30]

---

[29] Williams in his footnote adds: "This continuance in prayer is in the present participles, often repeated." Charles B. Williams, The New Testament in the Language of the People (Nashville: Holman Bible Publishers, 1986 edition), p. 159.

[30] Psalm 40:7,8; partially quoted in Hebrews 10:7.

CHAPTER

# The Astounding Prayer Life of Jesus

## Time to Begin

Jesus knew it was time to begin. The news of a prophet preaching and baptizing at Jordan had spread like a prairie fire throughout Galilee, Samaria, and Judea. John the Baptist was leading Israel in a great demonstration of repentance, declaring that "the kingdom of heaven is at hand."[1]

This was the signal that Jesus had waited for. Now, at the age of thirty, He made His way to the Jordan River. Humbly submitting to John, Jesus was baptized. Luke's Gospel adds the significant notation that He prayed:

Now it came about when all the people were baptized, that Jesus also was baptized, and while

---

[1]   Matthew 3:2.

He was praying, heaven was opened.[2]

This simple statement established that Jesus was already a person of devotion and prayer before He began His dynamic public ministry. The example of Joseph and Mary, the daily telling of Scripture stories, the training in the local synagogue --all contributed to His prayerfulness.

As a growing child in Nazareth, Jesus grew and "the grace of God was upon Him."[3] In His teenage years and young adulthood He was "in favor with God."[4] These expressions, I believe, indicate a strong prayer communion with the heavenly Father.

As He prayed in the Jordan River, the era of the Spirit was launched; the Father baptized Him with the Holy Spirit even as John baptized Him with water. Then He went to the wilderness.

And Jesus, full of the Holy Spirit, returned from the Jordan and was led about by the Spirit in the wilderness for forty days, while tempted by the devil. And He ate nothing during those days; and when they had ended, He became hungry.[5]

Although it does not say that He prayed in the wilderness, it must certainly by assumed. Matthew records that He was fasting,[6] so we know that He prayed. One may

---

[2]  Luke 3:21.

[3]  Luke 2:40.

[4]  Luke 2:52.

[5]  Luke 4:1,2.

[6]  Matthew 4:2.

pray without fasting (abstinence from food), but one does not fast without praying.[7] Fasting is the most intense and absorbing kind of prayer.

If our contention is correct that Jesus began each day with prayer, it seems strikingly significant that He also began His entire ministry with many days of continuous fasting and prayer. The devil could not break the will and determination of the Man of Prayer. Although exhausted and depleted, the Son of God overcame the temptations by the devil with Scriptures born in His heart through times of prayer.

We cannot assume that Jesus was being tempted continuously for forty days. The time surely was mainly devoted to communion with God and the appropriation of Scripture in prayer. The use of the Bible in intense intercession is common to great prayer warriors. This time in the wilderness set Jesus' course by placing God and His Word above any selfish inclinations, and in turn shows us the true foundation of all ministry. I like Dick Eastman's statement, "Without the Word, our prayer has no foundation."[8] His dynamic expression "Word Praying" seems to capture the activity of prayer and the Word that would characterize Jesus' food for forty awesome days. Possibly it was at this time that the Servant Songs of Isaiah became sharply focused in the mind of Jesus, bringing clarity to His destiny.

## Jesus' Personal Prayer

In combining the four Gospels I find a possible twenty-one to twenty-four different times when the record states that

---

7   Note how Jesus tied fasting and prayer together in Matthew 6:5-18.

8   Eastman, *Change the World*, C-19ff, Part VIII, "Word Praying".

Jesus prayed. He also taught much on prayer, of course, but the purpose in this chapter is to mention the actual instances of prayer.

Significantly, the second mention of His personal prayer occurs in the beginning of the Galilean ministry. The miracle power associated with the kingdom of God is being profusely demonstrated. The sick are being healed and devils are being cast out. With such wonderful results it would hardly seem necessary to pray very much, but His success only compels the Son of Man to prayer.

> And in the early morning, while it was still dark,
> He arose and went out and departed to a lonely
> place, and was praying there.[9]

Another astounding text confirms this attitude of Jesus. In the midst of the multitudes being healed, including a leper and a paralytic, Jesus prays. Luke's careful statement in 5:16 indicates Jesus' prayer times were habitual: "But He Himself would often slip away to the wilderness and pray." Luke additionally notes in the next verse that "the power of the Lord was present for Him to perform healing." The power cannot be disassociated from the prayer.

Luke says more about Jesus' prayer life than any other writer. As a physician he had a deep interest in the way his Master functioned. He shows us Jesus as the ideal Son of Man in various settings, but He particularly shows a fascination in the prayer life modeled by Jesus.

On one occasion Jesus dramatically heals a paralytic's hand on the Sabbath. The enraged scribes and pharisees plot to destroy Him. What does Jesus do in the face of such hostility?

---

[9]    Mark 1:35.

And it was at this time that He went off to the mountain to pray, and He spent the whole night in prayer to God.[10]

This undoubtedly accounts for the divine "power...coming from Him and healing them all."[11] At this point we see not only early morning prayer, but also all-night prayer.

In a sense, morning prayer is like the old-fashioned "priming the pump." Although the handle of the pump can be exercised, no water will flow until some water is poured down the shaft; then, water comes every time you push the handle. Jesus certainly prayed throughout the day, but the start of the day was of particular importance to Him. It would seem that since all of us do not pray as much or as strenuously as Jesus, we should at least give special attention to the proper spiritual start of our day.[12]

Luke chapter eleven is one of the most enlightening chapters of the Bible on prayer. This remarkable flow of information came because one of the disciples, obviously impressed by Jesus' prayer life, asked a simple question:

And it came about that while He was praying in a certain place, after He had finished, one of His disciples said to Him, "Lord, teach us to pray just as John also taught his disciples."

The way in which Jesus prayed must have been imposing. Just enough is said about the posture and place of His praying

---

[10]  Luke 6:12.

[11]  Luke 6:19.

[12]  Note that Daniel prayed regularly three times a day on his knees (Daniel 6:10), and David praised the Lord seven times a day (Psalms 119:164).

that we know a little of His intensity and fervency; as, in the Garden of Gethsemane when He fell to the ground on His face and prayed.[13]  The Gospel record certainly shows us a Man fluent in prayer at any time; He seems to live in a cloud of spiritual incense.  In the midst of His last public discourse, for instance, Jesus cries out:  "Father, glorify Thy name."[14]

Parents were eager to bring their children so that they might come under the influence of His prayers:

> Then some of the children were brought to Him so that He might lay His hands on them and pray.[15]

Adults should know that children learn more about prayer by watching and listening to adults pray than any other way.  How else will they learn?  There have been times when I have been praying fervently in our pre-service prayer meeting (just before Sunday School) when I suddenly open my eyes, and behold! --a child is staring at me, watching my every move.  I have found that if the child will learn some basic mechanics, the spiritual power of the prayer developing within the child will later have a channel through which to flow. I went through a number of years in which I despaired that my children would ever get excited about congregational prayer. Now they are every bit as fervent as I am!  Learn to include the children.  Bless them, pray for them, model the words and postures for them.  It won't be long before they will be praying too!

---

[13]  Matthew 26:39.

[14]  John 12:28.

[15]  Matthew 19:13.

<u>They Called Him "Praying Hyde"</u>

Although we are discussing the prayer life of Jesus in this chapter, please permit a brief diversion to consider a young man of the nineteenth century whose celebrated prayer life was tremendously affected by Jesus' example. John Hyde, the American missionary to India in the late 1800s, is famous as one of church history's leading examples of prayer. He has been respectfully called "Praying Hyde" for the past century. While attending a meeting in Calcutta, one of his friends had opportunity to observe John's prayer habits.

> ...I noticed what Mr. Hyde was doing in his room opposite. The room where I was being in darkness. I could see the flash of the electric light when he got out of bed and turned it on. I watched him do it at twelve and at two and at four, and then at five. From that time the light stayed on till sunrise. By this I knew that in spite of his night watches and illness, **he began his day at five.**[16]

His results were astounding. In spite of his many hours in prayer, he successfully came to the point of leading four Indians per day to accept Jesus Christ. In some ways Hyde's methods were more extreme than most of us would consider, but the results speak for themselves, and when I would seek for an example of someone who might pray like Jesus prayed, I cannot help but turn to John Hyde.

Dr. J. Wilbur Chapman found that his meetings in a certain English town were not succeeding at all until a certain American missionary came to town and began praying. Phenomenal results began to occur immediately as Hyde prayed. In one of his letters Chapman described praying with

---

[16]  Francis McGaw, *John Hyde: The Apostle of Prayer* (Minneapolis: Bethany House, 1970), pp 54,55.

Hyde. One cannot help but wonder if this was the manner in which Jesus prayed.

> Almost instantly the tide turned. The hall was packed, and my first invitation meant fifty men for Jesus Christ. As we were leaving I said "Mr. Hyde, I want you to pray for me." He came to my room, turned the key in the door, dropped on his knees, waited five minutes without a single syllable coming from his lips. I could hear my own heart thumping and beating. I felt the hot tears running down my face. I knew I was with God. Then with upturned face, down which the tears were streaming, he said: "Oh, God!"
>
> Then for five minutes at least, he was still again, and then when he knew he was talking with God his arm went around my shoulder and there came up from the depth of his heart such petitions for men as I had never heard before. I rose from my knees to know what real prayer was. We believe that prayer is mighty, and we believe it as we never did before.[17]

Hyde is a challenging and inspiring example, but none of us will ever pray quite like Hyde did, or Jesus, or any other great person of prayer. We can, however, learn lessons from their dedication, and we can seek to find our own role in the most important ministry of prayer. Let us return now to our analysis of Jesus' prayer life.

---

[17] *Hyde*, pp. 62, 63.

## Prayer Before Dinner

Matthew records the two amazing times that Jesus miraculously multiplied loaves and fish so that the people might eat. Before feeding the 5,000 people he looks up toward heaven and blesses the food.[18] Jesus is always the Man of prayer doing what comes most naturally to Him; in this case, He talks to the Father about His daily bread (while 5,000+ people watch in awe). Where does Jesus get this daring, audacious, mind-boggling idea of multiplying loaves and fish? It was born through the simple conviction learned in times of prayer that the Father would supply His daily bread as it was needed.

Afterward, He sends the disciples by boat to the other side of the Sea of Galilee. Then Jesus "went up to the mountain by Himself to pray."[19] These solitary prayer times recharge His spiritual abilities and powers. Although He prays throughout the day, these special, undistracted seasons alone with the Father appear to be His favorite times.

Matthew, in chapter fifteen, then tells how He feeds 4,000 people. Again He gives thanks as He breaks the loaves and fish.[20] His thankful prayer is not a sigh of relief that the miracle occurs, but rather a grateful acknowledgment to the Father who abides faithful to the needs of His children. The followers of Jesus observe their role model as a person very conscious of and confident in God's provision. We have all heard people pray over food whose sincerity might be doubted. In contrast, can you imagine what it would be like to hear Jesus pray before eating?

---

[18]   Matthew 14:19.

[19]   Matthew 14:23; Mark 6:46.

[20]   Matthew 15:36.

56 ◆ AWAKEN THE DAWN!

## A Mountain Top Experience

Jesus one day asked His disciples who the multitudes thought He was.[21] They gave various answers, but Peter boldly proclaimed, "The Christ of God." The setting for this question and answer was prayer, "while He was praying alone." It may be that the question was a subject of Jesus' prayers at that time. Notice from this text that Jesus did have personal prayer when His disciples were close at hand.

Eight days later, Jesus took Peter, James, and John "and went up to the mountain to pray." During prayer Jesus becomes transfigured with dazzling light.[22] Returning from that prayer mountain, Jesus finds His frustrated disciples trying to heal a boy having violent seizures. Quickly ejecting the unclean spirit from the boy, Jesus also reprimands the disciples for their unbelief. Could it not be that Jesus' great faith at that moment was directly linked to His time of communion with the Father on the mountain? Apparently at a later time Peter comes to understand the importance of such prayer, for he tells the early Church that he and the other apostles must "devote ourselves to prayer, and to the ministry of the Word."[23]

## Brimming over with Joy and Assurance

The Gospels give us three beautiful examples of the spontaneous joy and blessed assurance that characterizes Jesus the Man of prayer. Consider first the time when He brings scathing accusation against the cities of Chorazin, Bethsaida,

---

[21]  Luke 9:18.

[22]  Luke 9:29.

[23]  Acts 6:4.

and Capernaum for not believing in Him. Suddenly He breaks out in joyful praise that God has revealed His will instead to humble people:

> At that time Jesus answered and said, "I praise Thee, O Father, Lord of heaven and earth, that Thou didst hide these things from the wise and intelligent and didst reveal them to babes..."[24]

The joy and assurance that radiates from Jesus as He savors the ways of God could only result from a life of prayer.

Remember how seventy of His joyful followers return from a great evangelism crusade, gloating that even the demons were subject to them because of His name? Again, Jesus knows great joy and assurance as He perceives God's purpose. Notice the similar wording here in Luke 10:21, and also note that He was inspired of the Holy Spirit:

> At that very time He rejoiced greatly in the Holy Spirit, and said, "I praise Thee, O Father, Lord of heaven and earth, that Thou didst hide these things from the wise and intelligent and didst reveal them to babes. Yes, Father, for thus it was well-pleasing in Thy sight."

A third example takes place at Lazarus' tomb. Deliberately taking His time, Jesus arrives too late to pray for His sick friend. Lazarus was dead, buried, and at the time of Jesus' arrival is physically decomposing. With much boldness Jesus tells them to remove the great stone which covers the entrance to the sepulcher. His prayer is based on revelation that had previously come during a season of prayer.

---

[24]   Matthew 11:25.

And so they removed the stone. And Jesus raised
His eyes and said, "Father, I thank Thee that Thou
heardest Me. And I knew that Thou hearest Me
always; but because of the people standing around
I said it, that they may believe that Thou didst send
Me."[25]

The fact that Jesus thanks the Father that He had already
heard Him clearly shows that Jesus had communed already
and knew God's will in the matter. His supposedly foolish
action becomes an actual outworking of the will of the Father
in kingdom power.

### Everybody Needs the Helper

Jesus had help in His praying. Think for a moment
about praying all night on a mountain. What inspires Jesus to
send His disciples off while He remains alone on a mountain
during the darkness of night? How does a person pray alone
for hours at a stretch? Admittedly, there must be an affinity
for God, a longing for His presence. A praying person must
have a strong belief system and deep-seated convictions. Such
a person, we say, has faith.

There is, however, another dimension that must not be
overlooked. I speak of the heavenly "Helper" whom we know
as the Holy Spirit. Long periods of prayer on a mountain (or
anywhere else) would be difficult, if not impossible, without
the aid of the blessed Holy Spirit.

Jesus could speak with great assurance to His disciples
about "the Helper" that would come to them when He Himself
had gone. Since He Himself had known the comforting,
strengthening assistance of the Holy Spirit, He gives an
enthusiastic endorsement to the Father's plan of filling each

---

[25] John 11:41,42.

of them with the same Spirit. Jesus relied on the Holy Spirit to help Him, and He knew that the disciples could too. He was pleased that their prayer life would be empowered by the Helper.

Jesus was silent on this subject until His last supper with the disciples. Five times in His message He tells of the Coming One who will replace Him as their Helper.[26] The King James Version uses the term "Comforter." The Amplified Bible draws in additional, meaningful terms to help us understand the Holy Spirit's function: Counselor, Helper, Intercessor, Advocate, Strengthener, and Standby. It seems that "Helper" is probably the best way to translate this wonderful word.[27]

Jesus now reveals the secret of His power: it is the Holy Spirit. Notice how closely He associates prayer with the Helper's activities. Six times in His message to the disciples He tells us to "ask" in prayer.[28] This intertwining of thoughts, the promised Helper and prayer, is too obvious to be overlooked.

Jesus has Himself been a Comforter/Helper to His disciples. He has walked with them, slept with them, gotten wet in the boat with them, put His arm around them, etc. All of this, however, has been on the outside. The new Helper will come and replace Jesus' physical "outside" presence with a Spiritual "indwelling" presence. The Comforter (Holy Spirit) will actually be the person of the old Comforter (Jesus) in a new, closer relationship.

---

26  John 14: 16, 17, 26; 15:26; 16:7, 8, 13, 14.

27  A delightful book that bears this out in a very practical way is Catherine Marshall's *The Helper* (Waco: Word Books, 1979).

28  John 14:13, 14; 15:7, 16; 16:23, 24.

Jesus was helped in prayer by the Holy Spirit. The early Church learns this dynamic secret and they too "pray in the Spirit" with wonderful results.[29] Start each day with prayer, assisted by the Helper, and see how your days will be filled with a wonderful communion with the heavenly Father.

---

[29] Jude 20; Ephesians 6:18; Romans 8:26.

CHAPTER

# Refreshment
# in the Morning

## Early Morning Grazing

A good shepherd has his sheep grazing on the dew-drenched grass before the sun rises.  Phillip Keller's *A Shepherd Looks at Psalm 23* is one of my favorite books; in fact, I read it once each year.  He supplies this interesting insight that adds strength to my cause for early morning prayer:

> Most people are not aware that sheep can go for months on end, especially if the weather is not too hot, without actually drinking, if there is heavy dew on the grass each morning.  Sheep by habit, rise just before dawn and start to feed.  Or if there is bright moonlight they will graze at night.  The early hours are when the vegetation is drenched with dew, and sheep can keep fit on the amount of water taken in with their forage when they graze

before and after dawn.[1]

Keller goes on to explain that dew is a clear, clean, pure source of water, and that "the silver droplets of the dew hanging heavy on leaves and grass at break of day" is a resplendent picture of the still waters mentioned in Psalm 23. Early-morning grazing in dew-drenched grass beautifully illustrates our early-morning times in prayer and the Word. Dew cannot be found at any other time of the day; even so, I maintain, there is a special presence of God experienced only by those who "awaken the dawn."

> In the morning, O LORD, Thou wilt hear my voice;
> In the morning I will order my prayer to Thee and eagerly watch.[2]
>
> I rise before dawn and cry for help;
> I wait for Thy words.[3]
>
> Let me hear Thy lovingkindness in the morning;
> For I trust in Thee;
> Teach me the way in which I should walk;
> For to Thee I lift up my soul.[4]

It seems most significant that God supplied Israel with His miracle bread early each morning (except the Sabbath),

---

[1]  Phillip Keller, *A Shepherd Looks at Psalm 23* (Grand Rapids: Zondervan, 1970), pp. 51, 52.

[2]  Psalm 5:3.

[3]  Psalm 119:147.

[4]  Psalm 143:8.

much the same way as a shepherd puts his sheep early to pasture. Exodus 6:14 says: "When the layer of dew evaporated, behold, on the surface of the wilderness there was a fine flake-like thing, fine as frost on the ground." This manna not only appeared with the dew, but it evaporated with the sun! The Israelites had to gather the manna early each morning (except the Sabbath), or they would go without. Whatever manna was left over to the next day turned foul, stank, and became infested with maggots. Think of it! For forty years they arose early to gather their daily bread. How the Church today would be affected if every Christian would rise early to gather spiritual bread in the presence of the Father!

These beautiful words appear in the Lamentations of Jeremiah:

> The LORD'S lovingkindnesses indeed never cease,
> For His compassions never fail.
> They are new every morning;
> Great is Thy faithfulness.
> "The LORD is my portion," says my soul,
> "Therefore I have hope in Him."
> The LORD is good to those who wait for Him,
> To the person who seeks Him.[5]

## Alone with God

For an hour...just me...and God... alone together. I think we all acknowledge that God fills the universe, and He knows every move we make and all the thoughts we think. But somehow it is different when you set the time, you make the date, you expect literally to rendezvous with Almighty God for an actual hour.

---

[5] Lamentations 3:22-25.

The idea that one can really sense the presence of God--yes, even talk to Him--seems far-fetched to some. To those of us who set such times alone with God, there is no question but that He is real, wonderfully real, even at times a feelable presence. An enjoyable article on this subject appeared in the *Readers Digest* of March 1984.[6] Barbara Bartocci describes her experience in "One Hour that Can Change Your Life." She tells of her first attempt of spending an early morning hour with God; finally, after fifty minutes the very atmosphere began to change, "as the ambiance of a house will change when someone you love is home." Then the family awakened, "But all through the rest of that day, I felt warmed by the memory of that love." She soon discovered, like all the rest of us, that an hour in prayer is not always attended with the same warm feelings, or atmosphere. Sometimes one simply waits and shares with God. Regardless of emotion, however, the hour becomes an indispensable part of one's life. The following testimony by Bartocci is confirmed by so many praying people that it seems appropriate to include it here:

> Through every crisis, I have found a quietness of soul in that hour with God. It gives me time to put things in perspective, to find God in every circumstance. Once I find Him there seems to be no problem that cannot be resolved.

My own early morning prayer vigils began from a sense of desperate need for God's guidance. Although successful by most ministerial standards, I found myself spiritually stalemating after pastoring for twenty-two years in the church which I had founded. I was a Spirit-filled man of God, but my communion with Him was not what I wanted. I am embarrassed to say that it was not easy to develop the habit of

---

6    Barbara Bartocci, "One Hour that Can Change Your Life," *Readers Digest* (March 1984), pp. 13-16.

starting the day with an hour in His presence. Now I crusade to win converts to this wonderful practice!

I started my ministry at the age of twelve playing the piano for my mother's Sunday School in a public housing development. I remember that certain hymns were chosen to be sung with monotonous regularity. One of them was "Sweet Hour of Prayer." I wondered then (and still do) why people don't actually pray for an hour if it is so sweet. Thank God, I now understand what the dear blind minister meant when he penned that poem.

When a person first desires to pray on a regular basis, there will be a few problems. Count on it! But, the desire coupled with a consistent discipline will eventually turn into delight. Much of my prayer in the beginning centered in asking God to help me know His will. I needed direction for myself and the church, so I adopted some of the Psalms to reinforce my own faith. There were times that I would audibly and forcefully pray some of these statements time after time. Eventually the prayers became my prayers as the Word of God worked in me. I cannot help but feel that such prayer became the wonderful foundation for all that has happened in my life since. If you too are seeking help and direction, try using the following Scriptures to upgrade your prayers.

I love Psalm 27. I have walked the floor many times, prayer-reading those magnificent lines. For several days, when I first started morning prayer, two lines of verse 11 became an obsession; these are not just David's words anymore, I claim them as my very own:

Teach me Thy way, O LORD,
And lead me in a level path.

This is also a life changing passage:

Make me know Thy ways, O LORD;

Teach me Thy paths.
Lead me in Thy truth and teach me,
For Thou art the God of my salvation;
For Thee I wait all the day.[7]

A personal favorite of mine:

Make me understand the way of Thy precepts,
So I will meditate on Thy wonders.[8]

Or, as the Living Bible states it:

Make me understand what You want;
For then I shall see Your miracles.

## Did Jesus Need to Pray?

One of the great mysteries of my teen-aged years was why, if Jesus is God, did He need to pray to God. I have since discovered that greater minds than mine have wrestled with that concept down through the ages.

My early conception of Jesus Christ was that He could not help but do everything right since He was so totally overshadowed by divine power. It was as though some powerful prophetic inspiration rested upon Him; He could not sin, and His teaching was programmed directly from the Father in heaven.

I see the life of Jesus more clearly now. It still remains

---

[7]    Psalm 25:4, 5; also, note verses 9, 12, and 14.

[8]    Psalm 119:27. Israel knew the acts of God, but Moses knew His ways; note Psalms 103:7; 106:13; 95:9, 10.

a mystery,[9] but the importance of Jesus' humanity is not overlooked. God chose to enter our world by sharing our humanity, by becoming one of us, and being like us.[10] This is a wonderful part of the redemption story.

The ministry of Jesus, it seems to me, developed out of both a divine, prophetic dimension and also a very human life-situation context. Did He always, automatically know the right thing to do and say? I have come to believe that the Gospels include His active prayer life to show us that in His humanity He both experienced and modeled the efficiency and effectiveness of prayer. Restrained by His humanity from unleashing the full power of God, Jesus was dependent on knowing and doing the will of God just as we are. His life of prayer was genuine and necessary, and shows us that the choice secrets of His teaching and the dynamic manifestations of His power did not originate with Himself but with Him who had sent Him--the Father. His actions and teachings sprang from personal encounters with God in prayer.

Jesus' keen perception of people and situations was born from His times of prayer, particularly His intercession concerning the kingdom of God and the will of God. His brief capsulized statement about the kingdom and will of God in the Lord's Prayer in most English translations does not do justice to the deep experience He felt: "Thy kingdom come. Thy will be done, on earth as it is in heaven."[11] A more dynamic interpretation is given by Brad Young, a Hebrew specialist: "May You continue establishing Your kingdom, and

---

9   Note 1 Timothy 3:16.

10   Hebrews 2:14-18.

11   Matthew 6:9.

may Your will be done."[12]

Jesus taught His disciples to pray in this way both by divine inspiration and practical experience! Day-by-day He awakened with the heart cry: "Continue Your work through Me to establish Your kingdom, and may I do Your will!" To pray like this each day is to release a wondrous flow of God's inspiration your way. Jesus could teach these truths because He had personally experienced them, adopted them, and lived by them.

My point is this: The third Servant Song shows us that Jesus was taught by the Father in His times of early morning prayer. As the concepts came into His mind, He tested them in the crucible of life situations. Jesus found that what He was told of the Father is indeed true. He learned to come under the rule of God and to do the will of God. He learned to pray in this way daily. What He said, then, to the multitudes came not only from heaven, but also from His heart, "Pray, then, in this way: Our Father who art in heaven, hallowed by Thy name. Thy kingdom come. Thy will be done."

### Secrets of Prayer

During an exciting two-week period, the Lord seemed to drop "secrets of prayer" into my heart. As I look back on my own experience, I can easily believe that Jesus received His insights in early-morning sessions with the Father. Each morning I jotted the thoughts down hastily as I prayed, taking up a page or two in the blank pages of the Christmas book given to me by my daughter.

**Secret #1: God Loves Secrets.** This truth may have

---

12    Brad Young, *The Jewish Background to the Lord's Prayer* (Austin Texas:  Center for Judaic-Christian Studies, 1984), p. 17.

occurred to Jesus while reflecting on Isaiah 26:20, a portion of which He quoted in this statement given in Matthew 6:6:

> But you, when you pray, go into your inner room, and when you have shut your door, pray to your Father who is in secret and your Father who sees in secret will repay you.

I have been astounded at how Scriptures have come alive to me during prayer times. I have been trained to study, and I like to study and do research, but I can say truthfully that more living truths come to me during prayer times than during straight study. I am sure that the secrets of Jesus came to Him in similar manner. E.M. Bounds says:

> We can learn more in an hour praying, when praying indeed, than from many hours in the study. Books are in the [prayer] closet which can be found and read nowhere else. Revelations are made in the closet which are made nowhere else.[13]

Jesus' above statement is well known, particularly in the King James language. We are told to go into our "closet" to pray. This term, unfortunately, conveys a strange, negative connotation to the average reader. As a child, for instance, I understood Jesus to mean a broom closet.

It has helped me to see how the word *closet* is translated in other versions: "your room" (New International Version), "a room by yourself" (New English Bible). The Living Bible gives the basic meaning: "Go away by yourself, all alone."

Jesus, of course, did not pray in broom closets, but He did understand and practice private, uninterrupted communion

---

13     E.M. Bounds, *Power Through Prayer* (Grand Rapids: Zondervan, 1974), p. 59.

with His heavenly Father. A secluded wilderness area[14], an unoccupied garden[15], or a mountain top[16] may seem like uninviting (even frightening) places to commune with the Almighty; nevertheless, it was in just such settings that Jesus learned the ways and thoughts of God. Our text was born out of real-life situations where Jesus found for Himself the deep pleasures and inspiration which resulted from such private devotional times.

Naturally, God is everywhere. Jesus, however, found that the Father is particularly, wonderfully, personally "there in the secret place" (New English Bible). He sees clearly what is done in the secret place, but most significantly He sees what is secret or privately important to you. Phillip's Translation says it like this: "Your Father who sees all private things...."

It seems very important to God and Jesus that we take time to have secret rendezvous experiences with the Father. This, then, becomes a foundational truth of prayer: your Friend from heaven (who has unlimited power and resources) desires to meet with you regularly in some private, secluded place where He can personally hear, evaluate and give help to bring your heart's desires to pass.

Like Jesus, we may all pray in various places. It is best, however, to find your own private place of prayer where interruptions are minimized. Under normal operating procedures, a consistent meeting place and time will reap rich dividends for your prayer life. God likes it. Jesus said so. You will find it to be so. And, you will find the early morning hour one of the best suggestions that you can come up with as far as the time of meeting.

Secret #2. Never Give Up! In Luke 18:1-8 we have

---

14  Luke 5:16.

15  Luke 22:41.

16  Luke 6:12.

one of Jesus' parables recorded. There is no mistaking the two points of the parable, for Luke says: "Now He was telling them a parable to show that at all times they ought to pray and not to lose heart." The Williams Translation states both points strongly; first, "how necessary it is for people always to pray," and secondly, "never give up."

We all tend to give up too easily. Jesus urges us to pray on even when it does not seem that an answer is forthcoming. Sometimes a person can feel that repeating a request shows unbelief. It may, but it need not. Jesus undoubtedly taught us this because He Himself repeated requests. One classic example is the three times in Gethsemane when He prayed to the Father and asked for the cup to be removed from Him.[17]

Prayer should not be meaningless repetition of words or phrases. In Asian countries heathen paste prayer requests to prayer wheels, which then are revolved continuously in order to insure a continuous constancy that hopefully will affect the attention of the gods. Jesus tells us to pray at all times and never despair, but He does want us to believe that we are actually being heard by God. Do not be discouraged in your devotional pursuit of a desired request.

My father was a career army man. He returned from overseas duty in the Second World War to find that his wife and two sons had become fervent Christians. This was a real shock to him, and also a shock to me to find that my father was not interested in becoming a "born again" Christian. Naturally my mother, brother, and I prayed. My feeble teen-aged effort to convert him was soundly resisted. We prayed and we prayed. Years rolled by. Finally, after about twelve years, I had the joy of seeing him kneel at the altar of the church which I pastored at the time. Prayer was answered! I'm so glad that we didn't give up. Truthfully, I had the least faith for his conversion of just about anything for which I have

---

[17] Matthew 26:44.

ever prayed. But the continual asking was not a problem to my heavenly Father, and the whole process (as I now view it) built greater faith in my life than if God had granted an instantaneous answer.

Jesus seemed to understand there is a schedule in the dealings of God. The Father, when given sufficient lead-in time and latitude to work, will bring the answer eventually and beautifully. To a fast-food generation who wants everything served up immediately, the prayer closet becomes a great teacher. I have learned the simple, profound truth that even if I do not have faith to see some miraculous answer come, the fact that I do have faith that I am being heard by God and that I am consistently coming to God expecting Him to work things out in His own inimitable way, gives God reason to reward me openly!

Secret #3. Prayer Is Tested. We are told that "God tempted Abraham."[18] Actually, the meaning is that God *tested* this man of faith. Abraham discovered that praying people are often tested with the sacrifice of hard-won answers to previous prayer. Abraham had a son that God had provided in his old age; this delightful boy was surely the answer to his prayers! Then God asked him to sacrifice this son, his only true heir.

Only God could conceive such a soul-wrenching test. It has been said that "whatever you cherish most will either be an idol or an offering." Such precious possessions often come only because of long seasons of prayer. Abraham's willing response became one of the classic cases of obedience in the Bible. "By faith Abraham, when he was tested, offered up Isaac."[19]

In prayer God plumbs the depths of a person's soul. Strange requests come to praying people, and often

---

[18]  Genesis 22:1-10, King James Version.

[19]  Hebrews 11:17.

remarkable responses are given. Abraham knew this to be his only son, yet he knew that God had promised to use the boy. His conclusion, therefore, was that God would need to raise him from the dead. Testing is not to antagonize, but rather it is for the tempering of the soul. Like heated iron dipped repeatedly in shockingly cold water, the tested prayer warrior is steel hardened to glorify his Maker.

My first pastorate was in Spokane, Washington. It was a difficult six years of ministry for a struggling, neophyte minister. I prayed a great deal for that city, often walking and praying in the woods in a great spirit of intercession. My intensity of prayer for that city was so great that I came to identify my life, my future--everything--in terms of ministry in that city.

One evening at the conclusion of a united service of churches in Spokane, while a number of people were praying at the front of the auditorium, I had a remarkable experience toward the back of the platform. While praying intensely in a standing position, I suddenly experienced a mighty awareness of God's presence. I literally crumpled to the floor as God spoke to me.

I know this may sound "spooky" to some, and I am certainly tolerant of those who find such communication hard to believe. All I know is that God does talk to people on occasion, and I am convinced He talked to me. I have been a Christian for forty-eight years, and I feel that God has spoken to me audibly maybe five times during my spiritual pilgrimage.[20] So it certainly has not been an everyday occurrence for me.

---

20 The words are clear and distinct, certainly unpremeditated. I don't know if I literally "heard" the words, or if they simply came into my mind. At any rate, the clarity and the message were undeniable and not of my own making.

The most startling part of His message to me was:
"...your ministry in Spokane is finished." Alone, at the rear of
the platform crying and sobbing on the floor, I asked the Lord
in child-like manner: "Lord, what do you want me to do?"
The answer was astounding: "Go to San Jose and start a
church." A few minutes passed, and as I lay there in my tears,
the main speaker of the meeting, whom I hardly knew, came
over to me. Kneeling, he laid his hands upon me and said
words that were both confirmatory and prophetic: "If you will
do what God is laying on your heart to do, it will mean the
enlargement of your ministry...."

It has been an exciting adventure ever since. Joy and I
have been pastoring thirty-one years now in San Jose. I
thought I would live the rest of my life in Spokane. I thought
I would die there. My prayers and my faith were set. By
responding, however, to God's testing, it has literally meant an
unbelievable release for God's potential in my life. My friend,
don't be afraid of the challenges spawned by your life of
prayer. Let your idols become your offerings and great things
will result.

CHAPTER

# Deep Personal Satisfaction, Joy and Power

### It's a Good Feeling

One morning I awoke in Jerusalem! Joy and I were taking a tour of the Holy Land, and it was our first day in the ancient city. Being from California, my "time clock" still was not yet adjusted to Israeli time, so I found myself awake earlier than usual. I decided that I might as well get up and pray for an hour.

Looking out the window of our fourth floor room, I saw that all was quiet on the streets below and on the grounds of the Albright Institute across the street. After some time of prayer a strange sound startled me. It was a high pitched recorded voice of an Arab calling out through a loud speaker to that section of the city that it was time for Islams to pray. I believe it was about 5:20 a.m. I smiled to myself and thought, you are late this morning, Mohammed, the Church has already been in prayer for some time!

Jerusalem is indeed a praying city. Jews, Christians, and

Moslems all carry on an intense prayer ministry in this sacred place. Many American Christians have not yet learned what Islamic followers have known for centuries: religious conviction is maintained and heightened by periodic times of fasting and daily times of fervent prayer.

I cannot explain this feeling that one develops who regularly has early morning prayer. The joy and power of that meeting is so profound that the aura of it lingers throughout the day. It is a feeling of confidence, assurance, and of great dependence. Certainly it is not a critical attitude toward others who might pray less, but rather a deep, personal satisfaction and a sincere desire to see everyone experience the joy of His presence.

I remember so well the magnetic power in the TV messages of Bishop Fulton J. Sheen. An awe-struck young minister asked the bishop why he had so much more power in his ministry while he himself had so little. The response was tender and compassionate, but still unwaveringly firm: "If you would spend two hours each day in prayer as I do, you would also have power!"

This morning as I returned from praying at our church sanctuary, the sun was breaking over the eastern foothills of San Jose, California, where I live. I felt at that moment just as I had felt in Jerusalem: a deep satisfaction that my day is already given to God--I had awakened the dawn! I go forth with the "Son of righteousness" beaming His shafts of blessing down upon my life.[1]

## First Things First

In most time management courses a marvelous secret is shared that can transform a person's efficiency. It is so simple, so workable, and yet so consistently neglected. I mentioned

---

[1] Malachi 4:2, King James Version.

this earlier, but please let me repeat it:

> Each evening, write down all the important things that must be done tomorrow; now, number them in the order of their importance. Tomorrow, work on the most important things first. If you cannot do everything that day, you will at least have the satisfaction of knowing that you have done the most important things on your priority list.

Working at this concept has been of as much practical worth to me as a college education. I first heard of this idea many years ago while reading about Charles Schwaab, the president of Bethlehem Steel. Addressing management consultant Ivy Lee, Schwaab said: "Mr. Lee, I want to get more things done, and I'm willing to pay anything within reason." Mr. Lee pulled a three-by-five card out of his pocket and handed it to Schwaab. "I want you to write down the things that need to be done tomorrow, in the order of their real importance. When you come to work tomorrow, I want you to work on number one until it is completed. At the end of the day, write a new list. Try this system as long as you like, then have your staff try it. Evaluate this activity, and send me a check for what you think it's worth."

A few weeks later, Mr. Lee received a check for $25,000!

For maximum results (both spiritually and practically), make number one on your daily list an hour of prayer at the beginning of the day. Ordinary businessmen feel that "The assessment of daily priorities should be the first order of business each day."[2] I agree, but, bring your day under the covering of the kingdom of God through prayer. As you pray present to God the people, problems, events, and situations

---

2   See, for instance, Joseph D. Cooper, *How To Get More Done In Less Time* (Garden City:  Doubleday, 1971), p.5.

represented in your prioritized schedule for the day. As you pray, ask God to guide you and help you do His will. Pray for your specific plans as well as your unexpected interruptions.

At times you will feel certain impressions about the coming events. You may feel that certain rearrangements should be made. Learn to trust these thoughts that come to you in prayer; it is probably the Holy Spirit guiding you. Listen for God's guidance, and then obey. You are now "awakening the dawn" in the sense that you are bringing your day under the authority and blessing of the Almighty. This is administration by prayer; it should be the specialty of Christians.

It certainly appears that Jesus regarded personal prayer as of first importance. His life and ministry were shaped by the time management concept of Isaiah 50:4,5. He was given wisdom and insight and He learned how to minister successfully to the weary; His spiritual sensitivities were awakened; He was enabled to perceive the will of God and persevere in that will even when such action would be personally painful. All of this sprang out of His daily awakening into the presence of His Father. When Jesus told His disciples in the Sermon on the Mount to "seek first the kingdom" He was sharing a life style that He had proven over and over again.

## More Treasure from the Closet

In the last chapter I shared three "secrets of prayer" that God has made real to me through early morning prayer. I would like to share some more with you now.

**Secret #4.** He Seeks Your Welfare. Somehow we get the idea that we must zealously seek God because everything depends on just how earnestly and truly we pray and deny ourselves. Early morning prayer has persuaded me that God is seeking my welfare much more assiduously than I am seeking Him.

Going back to the Matthew 6:33 text, we find that many wonderful things will come to our lives if we put the Lord first. The Father Himself seeks to bless us and provide for our every need. His concern for our safety and well being is actually beyond our ability to comprehend. Let me state it as a principle: No matter how diligently I may seek Him, He already is more seriously seeking to bless and help me.

We humans seem to have a frustrating inclination toward drifting away from His will. This makes it difficult for the Lord to work with and bless us. It reminds me of a horse I once observed at the 4th Cavalry herds at Ft. Mead, South Dakota. My father was stationed at this last outpost of the military horse. I was in the fifth grade at the time, and my delight was to go out and ride herd with the men under my father's command. There was one horse that always strayed away from the rest of the herd. They told me it was because he was blind in one eye. He always faced the herd with his blind eye, so he never had the other horses in view; naturally he drifted away from them as he sought greener pasture. That horse was always off where he was not supposed to be, a constant irritation to those who were commissioned to his care. Let us keep out sights on God's will, and things will go much better for us!

I think many of us do have a blind side: we fail to recognize God's great desire to bless and prosper us. Our heavenly Father not only loves us with an invisible, spiritual love, but His love is very practical as well. He is deeply concerned that we are adequately provided with food, drink, clothing, and health. The remarkable assurances given by Jesus for these temporal things in Matthew 6:25-24 indicate first-hand conclusions drawn from His own prayer life. Five times in this text Jesus urges us not to be anxious about these things that the heathen so eagerly seek.

Instead, we are to seek continuously[3] the rulership and holiness of God in our lives. We are to make it a constant practice of seeking, and it is to be the priority item of all our desires and seeking. When we diligently seek Him, we release Him to bless us as He wishes.

King Uzziah's story in 2 Chronicles 26 provides a graphic illustration of this point. The man was blessed far beyond what he could have hoped for. Then he began to diminish his reliance on God and started to trust in his own strength. He was reduced from being a prosperous ruler of one of the great kingdoms of his day to a wretched man dying of leprosy under God's judgment. Verse five sums it up succinctly: "as long as he sought the LORD, God prospered him." God sought the man's welfare--but was rejected!

**Secret #5:** God Causes Good. Romans 8:28 is a verse that has brought a great deal of assurance to God's people:

> And we know that God causes all things to work
> together for good to those who love God, to those
> who are called according to His purpose.

God causes people, things, and circumstances to come into our lives that ordinarily would not come. These special, good things that will enhance and beautify our lives will come to those who love God and share their futures with Him.

We should not assume that things will just fall into place, that the historical flow of things will automatically work out like it is supposed to. Also, we should not presume to take the control of our lives into our own hands, relying on personal ability to pull things off.

God delights in having us commit our ways and days unto Him. When we seek divine, kingdom righteousness and rulership, somehow this frees God to act in a most benevolent

---

3    The original text indicates it is to be a continuous action; as, Matthew 7:7 and Luke 11:9.

fashion toward us His children. To lay out before God our calendar schedule, the list of things to be done, the family and people problems--to look at these items with God, seeking His will and direction--releases God to give us His best. All things then flow (under His hand) with God's good blessing. He wants to do great, good things for His children.

The early morning hours are the ideal time to lay your projects before the Almighty. Deliberately bring all your requests to God in bold statements of confidence. Invoke His will, ask that kingdom righteousness be released in your life, commit your life and everything associated with it to the goodness of the Almighty.

Be like Hezekiah when he was frightened by the Assyrian army:

Then Hezekiah took the (Assyrian) letter from the hand of the messengers and read it, and he went up to the house of the LORD and spread it out before the LORD. And Hezekiah prayed to the LORD saying....And now, O LORD our God, deliver us from his hand that all the kingdoms of the earth may know that Thou alone, LORD, art God.[4]

That last sentence of the prayer was hard for God to resist. When we will get out of the way, God is then enabled to bless us abundantly.

Let us not be so insecure about God's intentions. As an example, we can understand how reasonable it is for a person to seek the very best medical help available to cure an illness, but we must go into heavy mental manipulations to justify simply praying for healing because we are not sure that God is at all interested in our health! We tend to assume that our own personal concern for health, prosperity, and blessing is

---

4    Isaiah 37:14-20; 2 Kings 19:14-19.

much greater than that of God for us. It seems that we can take care of ourselves better than God can!

Even when we pray and much time elapses without a visible answer, believe that God is causing everything to work for good in your life. As I look back over the forty-four years that I have been a minister, I must admit that the things I remember with the greatest joy and delight are the times when the going was tough and it seemed there was no way out. Driven to prayer, I cried to the Rock of Ages. Never once did He fail me.

When we were building our present sanctuary, we used a church bond company to help us raise the construction money. It supposedly was a good company because a number of California churches had used their services successfully. Right in the middle of construction and our drive to sell bonds, however, the company was indicted by the government and our collected funds were frozen! At the time we were meeting temporarily in a rented Lutheran church on Sunday afternoons.

"Six months," we told the Lutherans, "We'll only use your facilities for six months, and then we will move into our new sanctuary." How hopeful we were!

When the government stepped in (supposedly to protect the people) we were truly thrown on the mercies of the Lord. The church felt like it was taking a torpedo midship! Finally. .. after three years. . .we moved into the completed sanctuary. How we prayed during those difficult days. We depended on whatever money we could get each week just to keep the construction going. It was like living from His hand to our mouths daily.

Now that I look at it all, it was one of the most wonderful times of my life. God really does cause good. Sometimes He manipulates these situations so that an even greater good will be accomplished: dependence on Him that He might work in our behalf.

**Secret #6:** Make Your Requests with Thanksgiving.

Thankfulness is a pleasant state of mind. It implies both gratitude for something and to somebody. Since thankfulness is mentioned so consistently with prayer, it may be the highest form of expressed faith. To appreciate and be grateful for something as yet unmaterialized must evoke in God the most pleasant of feelings.

One of the things I wrestled with the most in the first years of early morning prayer was the troublesome problem of ministerial competitiveness. If you are a business person, a homemaker, a student, I am sure that you have certain people who are a real irritation in your life. Please identify with me in my vocational problem, and see if the application will not work also in your life situation.

I am truly embarrassed to even bring this up, but this sixth secret has meant so much to me that I must share how God worked in prayer to change my heart. It should not be so, of course, but pastors often worry too much about the other churches and preachers in town. One hears a report of great blessing in the church across town; what do you do with a report like that? Especially, when you feel so deeply that your church is more spiritual(?!). Two things brought me out of that quagmire.

First, in my study of prayer, I was impressed at how often Paul spoke of giving thanks for other Christians:

(I) do not cease giving thanks for you, while making mention of you in my prayers.[5]

I thank my God in all my remembrance of you, always offering prayer with joy in my every prayer for you all.[6]

---

5    Ephesians 1:16.

6    Philippians 1:3,4.

We give thanks to God always for all of you, making mention of you in our prayers.[7]

We ought always to give thanks to God for you, brethren.[8]

I thank my God always, making mention of you in my prayers.[9]

After reading such statements, there was only one thing left for me to do. I actually learned to lift my hands and thank God for people that bothered me. I discovered that it works for relatives too! Call people by name and literally say (out loud): "Thank you Lord for so and so. I appreciate what you are doing in him/her. Bless them abundantly to know and do Your will."

This concept of thanksgiving can work for all of us. Mothers, for instance, have born handicapped children and turned a tragedy into a wonderful victory by learning to give thanks. A man in our church found it nearly impossible to work under a certain woman supervisor. Prayers of thanksgiving for the situation brought a wonderful resolution to the problem.

We are to converse with God about people, things, and situations (some of which may be very troubling). Our requests, however, are to be immersed in the incense cloud of thankfulness. Our expression must not be just a frantic "thank you Jesus" type of praying. Thankfulness is not born out of hysteria, but instead is born in a heart that contemplates on the ways of the Almighty. Time in His presence, the bathing

---

7    1 Thessalonians 1:2.

8    2 Thessalonians 1:3; also 2:13.

9    Philemon 4.

in His love, the sharing of His secrets. These things affect our hearts and the effectiveness of our prayers. This kind of praying requires at least a little time; hence, it is a plant that grows best in the climate of early morning prayer.

A kind, grateful child is such a pleasure to his parent. A higher form of love is evoked when the bonding element is thankfulness. Since God looks with loving gratitude on His creation and people, He is particularly pleased with He sees each of us bringing our prayers into His perspective. Have you ever contemplated what would get your prayers answered fastest?" I know this is not true, but it serves to make my point. Imagine our prayers like phone calls being handled by heaven's switchboard. Every caller is like a small light on the darkened planet Earth. There are thousands of little lights throughout the world. Which calls will receive immediate attention? I have no Scripture to back this up, but it seems to me that prayers connected with thanksgiving are so rare and so special, they are given priority status in heaven. What a change this secret has made in my life. Try it, I think you will notice an immediate difference.

Incidentally, those ministers that used to be thorns to me? They are now my best friends and we pray together regularly!

Secret #7: Verbalize Your Prayer. You will not find quiet prayer mentioned very much in the Bible. When I first discovered this I was really startled! Go through the entire book of Psalms and note every mention of prayer. You will find dozens of references that connect prayer with verbal expression. For instance:

> Lord, hear **my voice!**
> Let Thine ears be attentive
> To **the voice** of my supplications.[10]

---

[10]    Psalm 130:2.

There certainly is benefit in quiet times of prayer, but is it not a mistake for me to ignore all the Scriptural admonitions to use my mouth? Private, uninterrupted prayer lends itself to verbal expression. Do not be afraid to use your voice.

Jesus Himself learned this secret and practiced it much. How else would we know the words He used in Gethsemane in John 17? The disciples heard the Master use His voice in prayer. Jesus told His disciples to pray "saying."[11] We are aware that He taught that out of the abundance of the heart the mouth speaks. This principle involves not only the bad but also the good, and it also applies to prayer. Confession comes from the heart, but through the mouth.[12]

I have been pleasantly surprised to discover some things in Psalms that we are actually directed to say in our prayers. These expressions make prayers dynamic! Literally say them, repeat them, declare them:

Let all who seek Thee rejoice and be glad in Thee;
    Let those who love Thy salvation say
    continually,
"The LORD be magnified[13]

When Thou didst say, "Seek My face," my heart said to Thee,
"Thy face, O LORD, I shall seek."[14]

But as for me, I trust in Thee, O LORD,

---

11    Luke 11:2.

12    Romans 10:9.

13    Psalm 40:16.

14    Psalm 27:8.

I say, "Thou art my God."[15]

Let them shout for joy and rejoice, who favor my
vindication;
And let them say continually, "The LORD be
magnified,
Who delights in the prosperity of His servant."[16]

Verbalize these statements in magnifying God, and you
will find His power (strength) simultaneously released in
yourself. The human personality, reacting like machinery to
oil, functions best when it rejoices in God and His greatness.
Our thought patterns should pulse along channels which
joyfully announce that God is truly wonderful. Out of
abundant hearts our mouths should ceaselessly declare that
God in every circumstance of life is to be magnified.

---

[15]   Psalm 31:14.

[16]   Psalm 35:27.

CHAPTER

# On The Potter's Wheel

### Working the Clay

Like Jeremiah, we all need to visit the potter's house.[1] The deft hands working the moist clay have a vital message for all of us. As the glob of clay on the wheel begins to turn, the skillful potter fingers the clay and shapes it into some vessel of use and beauty. We are similarly shaped by the fingers and tools of God. Seeking to know God's will, we are like unformed clay on the revolving wheel of preparation. It is prayer, however, that is the tool of the great potter which molds us into vessels of honor. Mark well this law of the kingdom: The Holy Spirit uses prayer to work and shape our lives.

In this chapter I would like to suggest how prayer shaped the life and ministry of Jesus, and how this same process will work in us. It would seem impertinent to presume the full

---

1      Jeremiah 18.

details of the development of our Lord's experience of prayer; however, the carefully recorded facts of Jesus' words and anguished experiences in prayer, His example in prayer, and His teaching on prayer indicate that the intent of the Father is indeed for us to examine this sacred concept of Jesus' private prayer. Forgive me if at first I seem to presume too much, but also see if you too will not come to confirm and even experience the nine concepts which are presented in this chapter and the one following.

## First Importance

Concept 1. Jesus regarded personal prayer as of first importance. There is no question but that Jesus put His communion with the heavenly Father at the very top of His priority list of things to do. His communion with the heavenly Father was as necessary to His spiritual life as breathing is to the human body. His ministry was rooted in a life of prayer, and all that He accomplished was merely the fruit of a tree that drew its full sustenance from the soil of God's presence.

In a day when ministers and religious workers seem more inclined to work long and hard first (considering prayer as an afterthought), the life of Jesus presents a shining example of the very highest order of prayerful, ministerial service. It was not that Jesus neglected hard and long work, for He was most certainly a worker *par excellence*. The wonder of Jesus and His ministry was that He was shaped, motivated, and sustained by an astounding, dynamic personal life of prayer.

I wish I could relive my ministerial life. I probably would still work hard, but I would work smart. I would pray more, obey more, and trust more. I would not talk about prayer, read about prayer, attend prayer seminars, and preach on prayer without actually praying.

When a person practices the priority of prayer, God's mighty force is released to work. But, it is not just the answering of prayer that is important, it is the redirecting of life forces and ministerial ambitions that is most significant. The attitude about, the belief in, and the resultant rescheduling of life style to accommodate actual prayer, cause change in a person's life. Surely, Jesus' entire life was set in order by His profound conviction that personal prayer is of first importance. We can easily imagine how differently and ineffectively Jesus would have lived and ministered without this shining concept to guide Him. This life style is also within our reach, for the Master taught us to seek first.[2] Early morning prayer, prayer that begins our day, is an admirable way to implement this law of first importance. The other day I asked the group of people gathered for early morning prayer in our church sanctuary if they were discouraged about coming for prayer. I was not prepared for the enthusiastic endorsements that poured forth. They have found, just as I have, that starting the day with prayer is a priority that must not be given up!

## The Discipline of Private Prayer

Concept 2. Jesus maintained a discipline of private prayer. He not only believed in the priority of prayer, He so ordered His personal life and affairs that He was actually able to pray! To be consistent in prayer day by day, it is essential to frame a personal discipline of time and place. Otherwise, things will crowd in upon you, and time pressure will steal your prayer time.

I wish that I could say that getting up for early morning prayer gets easier as time passes, but that does not seem to be true of anyone I know. Those of us who do it, are excited and elated at the actual time of prayer, but facing the challenge of getting out of bed is not particularly exciting. It reminds me

---

2    Matthew 6:33.

of the old song, "Oh, how I hate to get up in the morning! Oh, how I hate to get out of bed...."

The best way to conquer the problem is to make certain arrangements the night before. It really helps me to lay out my clothes and toiletry articles. I have lived most of my life without a clothes valet, but now I have one. If everything is hanging in place and laid out, and you know where you are going and what must be done, it will help you get out of bed. You quickly and efficiently move through your morning getting-up routine, dress quickly, and then present yourself before the King.

This effort of discipline will reflect throughout your whole day and effect the very way you think. The maintenance of a discipline of private prayer, particularly early morning prayer, over an extended time will shape your life and ministry in a most profound way. The discipline of prayer will stimulate and produce the continuous life of prayer. Let us quickly review Jesus' prayer life by reading two paragraphs from a favorite book on prayer by Reginald White:

> And how He prayed! At His baptism, as He made His full response to the call that had come to Him, He Prayed; in the busy, crowded days in Galilee, rising a great while before day to be undisturbed, He prayed; in the wilderness, snatching another rare opportunity for quiet, He prayed. As He brake the bread for the multitude, and afterwards when some would forcibly make Him king, He prayed; before choosing the twelve, again when at Caesarea Philippi He questioned them about the progress of the work, and when they returned from their mission to the villages, He prayed. Heading southwards for the final challenge to Jerusalem, He lingered among the hills in Galilee for prayer and was transfigured and fortified.

As Peter faced his own testing-time, **Jesus prayed**; and in the Upper Room **He prayed** for them all. Before distributing the sacramental bread **He prayed** again, and later in the Garden facing out the full horror of the cross, three times **He prayed**. And as He had lived in constant prayer, so He died--"Father, forgive them...Why hast Thou forsaken me?...Father, into Thy hands..." All this, be it noted, is remembered and set down, though the record is far from complete, and a habit so constant called for little repetition in the story.[3]

### His Regular Response

**Concept 3.** Prayer was Jesus' regular response to situations of crisis and decision. There will always be unexpected interruptions in our lives. Problems, people, situations have a way of breaking in upon us uninvited and unscheduled. The natural tendency is to grapple with the intruder and solve the problem by keen evaluation and firm control. We think of Jesus and His serenity, so we then make the supreme mistake of trying to be confident and self-assured like our model Jesus, but without tapping into His source of strength!

Remember how the anxious sisters Mary and Martha summoned Jesus to come and pray for their dying brother? If they would have called me, I would have immediately ran to their aid and been unable to help them. Most of us are like that; we are well meaning, but misdirected. Jesus sorely disappointed the girls because He marched to a different drumbeat. In prayer He received some divine insight that came straight from heaven. He waited until Lazarus was dead

---

[3]     Reginald E. O. White, *They Teach Us To Pray* (New York: Harper and Brothers, 1957), p. 178.

and decomposing! Then He came and raised him from the dead. This wonderful action was the direct result of His responding to crisis with prayer.[4] These words of Henry David Thoreau hang on my wall and seem so descriptive of the person whose life is directed and managed by prayer:

> Why should we be in such desperate haste to
>     succeed,
>     and in such desperate enterprises?
> If a man does not keep pace with his companions,
>     perhaps it is because he hears a different
>     drummer.
> Let him step to the music which he hears,
>     however measured or far away.

We take too much for granted about the miracle of Jesus' peace, the calmness of His spirit, and the poise with which He conducted Himself. These attributes flowed from a life of prayer. His peace came from the Father of peace. On the night, for instance, that preceded the day when He would choose the Twelve, He spent the lonely hours in prayer; then, when He faced the entire company of followers He chose unerringly the apostles with an assurance that could only come from heaven.

What would the average pastor do if he knew that on a certain day of teaching there would be present in his audience church leaders, seminary professors, and leading theologians? I probably would spend all my time polishing up my thoughts, doing research for choice, impressive information, and practicing the right gesticulation and articulation. Jesus, in a similar situation, apparently did not worry about explaining the kingdom of God; instead, He proceeded to amaze the Pharisees and doctors of the law ("which were come out of every town of Galilee, and Judea, and Jerusalem") by

---

4    John 11:41, 42.

demonstrating the kingdom. This was a direct result of withdrawing Himself into the wilderness and praying; Luke records the event in profound simplicity: "and the power of the Lord was present for Him to perform healing."[5]

## The Distinctive Word "Abba"

**Concept 4.** The distinctive word "Abba" characterizes the Father-Son relationship that Jesus enjoyed and shows how His emotions and faith found clearest expression. The average English reader of the Bible finds certain words hard to understand, even when explained. I had this trouble with the word "Abba." My research helped me academically, but not emotionally! I learned that the word was an Aramaic form of the Hebrew, transliterated into Greek in the New Testament and then into English. I found that the word does not appear in either the Hebrew Old Testament or the Greek Septuagint Version of the Old Testament, but it does appear in three New Testament prayers.[6] I was helped by reading Ralph P. Martin's comment:

Abba is our Lord's favorite designation for God; and has been the subject of much scholarly research. We have the German scholars to thank for the conclusion that while Abba was the child's word for his earthly father, there is no evidence that the pious Jew ever used precisely this form (meaning 'dear father', 'daddy') of God. Instead, he used a variant form like Abinu, 'our Father'), but Abba was avoided because it was thought to be too daring and familiar an expression to be used of

---

5    Luke 5:16,17.

6    Mark 14:36; Romans 8:15; Galatians 4:6.

the King of the universe.[7]

The meaning really burst upon me, however, not in the library but in a public park in Jerusalem. Joy and I were admiring the general setting when suddenly a little Jewish boy came running across the grass. The dark-haired child in short pants looked very much like any American boy playing in the park. The words, however, which poured from his mouth started bells ringing in my mind! "Abba, Abba," he yelled. Running over to his father, the child lovingly threw his arms around his daddy's leg. As I stood there watching this typical family scene, I realized that Jesus surely was employing "a nursery word to convey the thought of God's fatherly love, care and provision for men and women as His children."[8] That picture has been worth 10,000 theological words to me!

Jesus obviously introduced a whole new concept of intimacy with the Almighty God. Apparently Paul and the early Church picked up this same terminology and same spiritual relationship that Jesus had modeled for them. In the Garden of Gethsemane Jesus cried out: "Abba, Father. . ."[9] Paul describes how the Holy Spirit of Jesus now continues that cry in our prayer times:

> For ye have not received the spirit of bondage again to fear; but ye have received the Spirit of adoption, whereby we cry, Abba, Father.[10]

---

[7] Ralph P. Martin, *Worship in the Early Church* (Grand Rapids: Eerdmans, 1964), p. 35.

[8] Ralph P. Martin, *The Worship of God* (Grand Rapids: Eerdmans, 1982), p. 35.

[9] Mark 14:36.

[10] Romans 8:15, King James Version.

The prayer life of Jesus produced an unusual intimacy with the Father. Furthermore, the early Christians passed on both the tradition and the experience of Jesus' prayer life. Dare we claim this wonderful intimacy for the Church of our day? Certainly we can!

Christians have become so harassed by time problems that the simplicity and power of prayer have been forgotten. It is as though the sands of time have covered over wondrous treasure that has been neglected when it should be used. The power of Jesus' prayer life lay not so much in an overwhelming spirituality as in a personal dedication to do those things that please the Father. Since communion with the Father seems to be of highest priority to God, those who will respond to His invitation will be amply rewarded, both with intimate experience as well as gloriously answered prayers.

Most commentators feel that the English word "Father," that Jesus uses so much in the Gospels, holds the same significant meaning as Abba. If this be true, we can easily see that Jesus' special way of teaching and ministering to people was the result of His Abba-praying. The love and authority of the Father was first experienced, and then out of this life-experience there poured the Spiritual rivers of living water. The base of Jesus' teaching is so different from that presented in the ministerial training centers. Whereas the rabbis of every generation prefer the academic handling of facts and history, Jesus brought and still brings a new and living way that springs out of the personal relationship gained through a life of prayer.

The sense of God to Jesus was so real, so loving, so compelling, the cry "Abba!" most naturally came to His lips in times of prayer. The term fell easily and without provocation from His lips in teaching as well. Jesus lived in an unusual, conscious intimacy with God, and this wonderful relationship was never taken for granted. Rather, it was fueled by a disciplined life-style of prayer that also found expression in spontaneous times of seeking God.

From time to time we meet people who are truly people of prayer. One senses in them this same consciousness and authority that we are talking about. No one can habitually come into the presence of God and remain unchanged. Not only did Jesus find His life and ministry shaped through prayer, but we too can know Him on intimate terms and find the same wonderful work of shaping and molding by the hands of the Master Potter.[11]

---

[11]     Isaiah 64:8.

CHAPTER

# A Vessel of Honor

### Reflections on a Rummage Sale

It was a bright, beautiful day in the city of San Jose, California. Ideal, certainly, for the bustling activity in our church parking lot. Rummage Sale! Our church people were excited, and neighborhood folks were stopping by. Truthfully, these events do not particularly excite me, but I usually put in my token pastoral appearance. (I always feel that somehow church people just transfer rummage from one family's garage to that of some other hapless family.) I strolled with interest from one table to another.

I like the tables that have used books. Stopping at one such table, I glanced over the titles. My eyes fell on a certain book, and I knew instinctively that I must have this book! The title bore the name of a man that has become synonymous with prayer and faith. Next to Paul and other Bible characters, this man is probably referred to in Christian periodicals, books, and sermons more than any other person.

I dare say that on a given Sunday in any large city, at least one preacher will mention George Mueller; I myself have used snatches of his life story to illustrate the power of believing prayer. So, when I saw the book, I knew the time had come for me to sit down and read carefully the entire story of George Mueller. With trembling hands I quickly made the purchase, fearful that someone would grab the book ahead of me!

In the late 1800s George Mueller lived a remarkable life of dedicated prayer and faith, housing and feeding thousands of homeless children in Bristol, England, advertising his financial needs to no one but God. The astounding results of George Mueller's relationship of delight and confidence in God have made his name a byword for faith throughout the world. "Indeed, it was to demonstrate what can be wrought by faith that Mueller originally began his work." His own statement is clear, concise, and very challenging:

> My chief object was the glory of God, by giving a practical demonstration as to what could be accomplished simply through the instrumentality of prayer and faith, in order thus to benefit the Church of Christ at large, and to lead a careless world to see the reality of the things of God, by showing them in this work, that the Living God is still, as four thousand years ago, the Living God....That it may be seen how much one poor man, simply by trusting in God, can bring about by prayer; and that thus other children of God may be led to carry on the work of God in dependence upon Him, and that children of God may be led increasingly to trust in Him in their individual

positions and circumstances....[1]

Mueller's life story encouraged me greatly. Early morning prayer was a vital part of his life, of course; prayer, in fact, permeated all that he did. The most insignificant things were brought to God in prayer. It was not unusual for large bills to be met on the last day, or the last hour, but always in answer to prayer. His testimony should encourage any reader of this book:

> If I say that during the fifty-four years and nine months that I have been a believer in the Lord Jesus Christ I have had thirty thousand answers to prayer, either in the same hour or the same day that the requests were made, I should not go a particle too far. Often, before leaving my bedroom in the morning, have I had prayer answered that was offered that morning, and in the course of the day I have had five or six more answers to prayer; so that at least thirty thousand prayers have been answered the self-same hour of the self-same day that they were offered. But one or the other might suppose all my prayers have been thus promptly answered. No; not all of them. Sometimes I have had to wait weeks, months or years; sometimes many years.[2]

The life of prayer shaped, fired, and produced of George Mueller's life a vessel of honor and beauty: an insignificant man made into a testimony of greatness that we doubt has

---

[1]     Roger Steer, *George Mueller: Delighted in God!* (Wheaton: Harold Shaw Publishers, 1975), pp. 157, 158.

[2]     Ibid., p. 246.

ever been equalled. Paul stated it all:

> Therefore, if a man cleanses himself from these
> things, he will be a vessel of honor, sanctified,
> useful to the Master, prepared for every good
> work.[3]

Although we are studying the principles which shaped
Jesus' prayer and ministry, it seems good to show that men
like Mueller have been able to incorporate such concepts into
their personal lives. Jesus' doctrine of prayer still works in our
day, and we too can shape our lives and ministries through the
power of prayer. In the last chapter we discussed four of the
nine concepts of prayer, now let's examine the last five.

### A Sense of Sonship

Concept 5. During times of prayer, Jesus' sense of
sonship became powerfully real as He experienced intimate
relationship with the Father. This acute awareness of God's
fatherly care was reflected in His public ministry.

Speakers and writers try not to repeat the same words
frequently. Jesus apparently felt no such problem in the
constant use of "Father" to substantiate His teaching and
claims. Jesus had a disconcerting way of talking personally
about His relationship with God that was absolutely
maddening to the religious leaders of His day. The Gospel of
John abounds with illustrations of this very thing. My
contention is that such statements were authentic
announcements which flowed forth from His times of prayer
and communion with the Father.

In His complicated teaching recorded in John chapter
five, Jesus uses "Father" fifteen times. How could He talk like

---

[3]     2 Timothy 2:21; also, Romans 9:21.

this? Did He learn it at the synagogue school? Did His religious teachers speak thus?

He spoke out of an awareness that came from real-life communion. In chapter six Jesus used "Father" nine times in explaining the bread of life. He talks about having the seal of the Father, the bread of the Father, knowing the will of the Father, being sent by the Father. He says he has "seen" the Father,[4] and John includes in his record that "the only begotten God, who is in the bosom of the Father, He has explained Him."[5] The Amplified Version makes "in the bosom of" to mean "in the intimate presence." A footnote from *The Life of Christ in Stereo* gives this insight:

> The Greek expression pictures two persons at dinner, ancient style, reclining with feet away from the table, one leaning against the bosom of the other at his left; the symbolism pictures complete fellowship.[6]

We must be cautious in discussing "Jesus' example in prayer." We are limited in how far we can follow Him into the power and depth of prayer. In one sense, we can claim the third Servant Song of Isaiah as our model, and yet we must face the great gulf between His prayers and ours. His personal prayer life was a standard of excellence beyond our capabilities, yet set before us as the ideal of our efforts. We

---

[4]    John 6:46.

[5]    John 1:18.

[6]    Johnston M. Cheney, *The Life of Christ in Stereo* (Portland: Western Baptist Seminary Press, 1969), p. 241.

recognize that He is one with us, but not one of us.[7] Our Lord was truly man, and as a man He needed to be in contact with the Father. He ministered as a man among men, and what He did as man was related to how He prayed as man. A good basic summary of this thought is given by Harold Lindsell:

> If the true man, who lived in sinless life, needed to have this prayer fellowship then sinful men are even more in need of this kind of communion. Therefore, if Jesus prayed it is necessary for everyone else to pray. And however much He needed prayer, as to time and effort spent in its exercise, His followers need it even more than He did. So the people of God should make prayer as central to their lives as Jesus made it to His....If the followers of Jesus are to do great exploits for God they must mirror the pattern disclosed in the life of Jesus, and that pattern has prayer for a central motif.[8]

In the eighth chapter of John Jesus defends His ministry, employing "Father" eight times. He knows where He is going, He speaks things the Father has taught Him (things which He has "seen"!), He argues that He honors the Father. Surely this strong sense of sonship originated and matured in the life of prayer.

It is no longer a secret to me why "the Lord's Prayer" begins with "Our Father." Prayer is a living communion, an actual interfacing with God. As children we speak with our Abba! This revelation changes a person's life. To be aware

---

7    Hebrews 2:14-18.

8    Harold Lindsell, *When You Pray* (Grand Rapids: Baker Book House, 1975 edition), p. 157.

of the Father's care is to reflect a ministry of divine love.

## Sharpening the Focus

**Concept 6.** The consciousness of *His ministerial commission* and the sharpening of its focus can be traced to His prayer life and the revelation that was a natural consequence of it.

Prayer does more to prepare a person for his or her life work and calling than anything else that can be done. This does not minimize education and training, it merely gives priority to finding God's will. A girl seeking a husband, a young man seeking a worthwhile profession, these and all other situations find their best solutions when we pray. The fuzziness of our lives will sharpen into clear focus when we pray.

Since I am a pastor, let me illustrate this principle from my own life. Prayer does more to prepare a person for ministry than anything else that he or she can do. Naturally a minister should know how to speak and have basic knowledge of life, history, etc. Unfortunately, however, we have hundreds of religious leaders who are in a profession by choice rather than by calling.

I remember how concerned I was as a junior and senior in college. At the age of fourteen, God had called me to be a full-time minister of the Gospel. By the time I was finishing my college work, however, I had a wife, a baby, household bills--and the pressure of all my ministerial student friends going off to seminary. I had talked to one of the students when I was a freshman in the dormitory at Whitworth College in Spokane. I spoke enthusiastically about the power of the Holy Spirit and he flippantly turned to me and said, "I don't need to worry about that now, they will explain that to me when I get to Princeton." Sometimes I think our awe of academic institutions borders on the deification of learning.

I watched my friends go off to Princeton, Dallas, and Fuller Seminaries. I found myself praying a great deal in those days. I had asked the Lord very directly if He wanted me to go to seminary. The voice of the Lord sounded in my mind so clearly, "You will go to seminary." During the three years I would have been in seminary, the Lord opened up a small church building in Spokane, and I began to pastor a handful of people.

One day alone in the sanctuary, I prayed earnestly, crying out: "Oh, Lord, I thought you wanted me to go to seminary." Again that still small voice came so powerfully and with such assurance: "You are in your seminary!" As my friends returned from their seminaries, there was invariably a great concern about where they would go to find a church that would accept them. I couldn't help but smile as I observed all of this, because I was pastoring in the place where I felt God wanted me because He Himself had opened the door.[9] Prayer had taken me along a road uniquely selected for me by my heavenly Father.

But. . . everyone is not called to be a full-time minister; in fact (in spite of all the teaching about spiritual gifts and ministries), most people will not be tremendous leaders. Most of us are followers who will have to function in the secular work place, balancing the problems of worldly and spiritual living, attempting to raise our families while trying to function in a hostile environment. I would like to encourage you to believe that this sixth concept will work for even you. You do indeed have a calling, a gifting, a ministry. Sometimes when

---

[9]   Finally I did earn an M.A. in Biblical Theology from Fuller Theological Seminary when I was in my fifties and had been pastoring where God wanted me in Spokane and San Jose. It took me nine years to earn a two-year degree! It was a different road, but I wouldn't trade this experience for the world.

I address our congregation my heart hurts as I see single parents trying to raise little children, older people with physical pain. Yet, each and everyone of us has a part to play in the advancement of God's great kingdom.

As you read my comments about Jesus, realize that prayer will affect you in similar fashion. You might consider combining your prayer with a very practical approach. For instance, take an evaluative book like *Discover Your God-Given Gifts* by Don and Katie Fortune,[10] and carefully analyze your vocation, your personality, and your desired ministry utilizing the diagnostic tools provided. The focus will start to sharpen for you if you can combine sincere prayer with such insightful analysis.

Prayer caused Jesus to realize who He was,[11] and prayer caused Him to see how certain Scriptures related to Himself (as in the four "Servant Songs" of Isaiah). Prayer sharpened His sensitivity to when and where He should go; such as the time "He had to pass through Samaria" to deliver the single greatest statement ever spoken on the subject of worship.[12]

In prayer Jesus developed a sense of authority that came from no seminary or rabbinical school. Learned theologians have this unique way of taking a text of Scripture and saying, "Now, this is an interesting thing about this text...." Not Jesus! He spoke out of a life-experience context. His message came from God like a hotcake right off the griddle. He spoke things, explained things, with an assurance born from prayer-communion with His Father. This alone can account for the

---

10   Don and Katie Fortune, *Discover Your God-Given Gifts* (Old Tappan, New Jersey: Fleming H. Revell, 1987).

11   John 8:42.

12   John 4:4; 4:21-24.

108 ◆ AWAKEN THE DAWN!

audacity of His public speaking. He would preface his remarks with "Amen," sometimes using the word twice for added emphasis. He would refer to what the Law had to say, and then, in what must have seemed impertinence to the Rabbis, He would declare, "but I say...." He would pronounce certain things "blessed." He would declare, "Behold!"

Certainly we should be scholarly and careful. There must be study! The point here is not to discredit preparation, but rather to plead for us to find the authority that comes only in the presence of the Almighty. I remember that I was so pleased to have studied New Testament Greek in college. On one occasion I tried to share the nuances of some word to a working man with marital problems. Dressed in suit and tie, I excitedly tried to explain things to my friend in baggy, dirty working man's clothes. The poor fellow had a glazed look over his eyes as I attempted to enlighten him on the fine points of some ancient Greek verb. Finally he had enough of my high falutin' lecture and he exploded: "I don't care about the Greek! Just tell me what the Bible says." Well, word studies are important, but the bottom line is whether we have an authority to heal the hurting. Jesus had it, because He awakened each morning to be taught of the Father.

One more thing about Jesus' ministerial consciousness. We might better call it "His eschatological consciousness." Jesus had a remarkable ability to maintain tension between the now and the later. He actually gave five of His key teachings in this confusing style: He talked of resurrection now, and yet to come;[13] the present scattering of disciples that will also be later;[14] worship in the Spirit that was now and yet future;[15] the kingdom of God that is now and yet to

---

[13]    John 5:25, 28; 11:25, 26, 43, 44.

[14]    John 16:32; Mark 14:27, 50; Matthew 24:9, 10.

[15]    John 4:23; Luke 10:21; John 7:39.

come;[16] and Satan's judgment, now and later.[17]

The timing of His doctrinal interpretation paralleled His ministerial activities. How did He get this perfect timing? For instance, as He walks triumphantly through Jericho, surrounded by an enthusiastic crowd, He stops to bring healing to the blind beggar Bartimaeus whose voice would have otherwise been lost in the cacophony of sound.[18] How does He know the sincerity of those who would be His disciples? How does He know when to start telling His followers about His coming crucifixion? Prayer is the framework of His operations. In prayer the Son of Man perceives both the nowness as well as the laterness of what He is doing and what He is teaching. Apparently, some things He knew ahead of time, other things came to Him immediately as the need presented itself. But, I maintain, it was in the context of prayer that the direction needed was provided.

I remember so well how this worked for me once. I had begun pastoring our church in San Jose. We were in our first building, the old 20th St. Church of God which we had purchased. The building was rundown, and the sidewalks were buckling. I was particularly concerned about someone getting hurt on the uneven walk. But we had no money, so I prayed about it.

One afternoon as I was driving home from the church, I felt impressed to turn the car in at the Purple Heart used clothing store. Actually, I was more than impressed, my hands spun the wheel before I realized what I was doing. I got out of the car, perceiving that for some reason I was supposed to be in that place which I had previously never entered. I walked in. I saw no one that I knew. Nervously, I went over

---

16    Luke 11:20; Matthew 25:34.

17    John 12:31; 14:30.

18    Mark 10:46-52.

to a candy machine and got something to eat to occupy my time. Then I felt I should look around. Walking down one of the back aisles I came upon a woman who attended our church. With her was her husband. The man was usually so nervous about preachers that he would run into the bathroom or out the back door whenever I called.

At this moment I caught him totally unprepared! He cheerfully asked me how things were progressing with the sidewalk situation. His wife had told him of our dilemma. He just happened to work for a cement company. Well, to make a long story short, he literally talked himself and his friends into delivering and setting the cement! Prayer was answered, but it hinged on obediently turning into a store that I had no desire to visit. Being prayerful prepares you for experiences like this.

## The Source of Devotion and Obedience

**Concept 7.** Jesus' devotion and obedience to the Father are a direct result of frequent communion with the Father. Somehow Jesus learned that His success was dependent on never initiating any projects of His own:

> I can do nothing on My own initiative. As I hear, I judge; and My judgment is just, cause I do not seek My own will, but the will of Him who sent me.[19]

> I do nothing on My own initiative, but I speak these things as the Father taught me.[20]

---

[19]   John 5:30.

[20]   John 8:28; also, 8:42; 10:18; 11:51; 12:49; 14:10.

It is impossible to explain this concept in detail, but I know that every praying person has learned the truth of it. The more we are in the Father's presence, the more we desire to do His will. This unusual passage in Hebrews 5:7, 8, bears out that Jesus Himself learned obedience though prayer:

> In the days of His flesh, he offered up both prayers and supplications with loud crying and tears to the One able to save Him from death, and He was heard because of His piety. Although He was a Son, He learned obedience from the things which He suffered.

## Deep Insight

Concept 8. The experience and intimacy in prayer gave Jesus His deep insight into: (1) the character and will of God, (2) the limitations of human nature, and (3) the character and strategies of His satanic adversary.

Amazing insights come when a person prayer-reads the Bible. Not only do we come closer to the literal, original meaning, but we also receive exciting applications of truth to our personal lives. To prayer-read the Psalms over an extended period of time has a revolutionary affect. The character of God, the attributes of God, the ways of God, all become so wonderfully real.

Another benefit is to see the futility of man's efforts. Our limitations are part of God's plan to make us dependent on Him. This is not meant to rob us of our self esteem, but rather to show us that our fulfillment lies in allowing the Almighty to be God of all that we are.

Prayer tuned Jesus in on Satan's strategies. Prayer brought to Jesus the absolute certainty of Satan's demise.[21]

---

[21]    John 16:11.

Jesus was so perfectly alerted to Satan's desires and designs, that He could declare: "And he has nothing in Me."[22] The many terms and titles that Jesus used of the devil indicate a spiritual discernment of His adversary that was born out of a life of communion with the Father. The Holy Spirit shows us how to do battle with our enemy. A good illustration is given in the story of the king of Syria who could not understand how his private strategy sessions were known by the king of Israel. The answer was simple: A prophet named Elisha listened in on the conversations through the power of the Holy Spirit.[23]

## Rendered Impervious

Concept 9. Prayer rendered Jesus impervious to the firey darts of Satan and calloused Him toward the enticements which accompany great popularity.

Jesus met His adversary during His time in the wilderness. Forty days of fasting and prayer had depleted His energies. Although exhausted in body, Jesus used the Word of God in powerful denouncements of the diabolical temptations hurled at Him;[24] Satan fled, and angels came and ministered to Jesus. Devils acknowledged Him to be the Son of God, but He had no time for their antics or ideas. Jesus set His course to do the will of the Father, and this He did by maintaining a wondrous prayer life and communion with the Father.

The crowds would crown Him king when they beheld His

---

22  John 14:30.

23  2 Kings 6:12.

24  Matthew 4 and Luke 4.

power to multiply bread and fish to feed 5,000.[25] Jesus, however, found it more blessed to abide in the Father's will, so He withdrew to a mountain to be alone. This kind of temptation frequently comes to Christians. Well-meaning people would rob us of our true calling by putting us on committees, running us ragged with things to do, keeping us from the all-important thing--prayer. It becomes so easy to feel that all of our activities, contacts, connections, and phone calls mean we are successful. We need to seek the heavenly Father earnestly as David does:

> O God, Thou art my God; I shall seek Thee earnestly;
> my soul thirsts for Thee, my flesh yearns for Thee,
> in a dry and weary land where there is no water.
> My soul clings to Thee; Thy right hand upholds me.[26]

---

[25] John 6:15.

[26] Psalm 63:1,8.

CHAPTER

# Working Out
# for an Hour

## Mirror, Mirror on the Wall

I just got back from the most intimidating place in town. Strangely, my goal is to visit this slave factory at least three days a week, but it takes all my effort to get my body there. I know that I will feel great after about an hour's workout at the Fitness Center, but it takes all the discipline I can muster to pull it off. Everything about the health spa is geared to bully and scare me into being a healthy, vibrant individual.

When I signed up, an athletic young man showed me around the twenty or so machines, helping check out my present muscle power for each apparatus. The poundage for each machine was carefully noted on my personal card. I now try to go in for about an hour or so three times a week, working out on a dozen machines, followed by two dozen laps in the pool. I feel great after all this, and I even think more clearly. Sedentary preacher-types need to exercise muscles besides their mouths. I asked myself, "Ernest, why should you die before your time?" No reason, I concluded, unless it would be lack of exercise!

I have two problems down there. First, it is these disgustingly healthy, muscular guys. When I get off a machine where I pushed eighty pounds, they walk over and plug in one hundred and eighty pounds! At sixty-one years of age, I figure I am doing fairly well. But these people who consistently work out and build up their strength--well, it just intimidates me to see what I might be if I would just work at it.

Secondly, the mirrors. They have mirrors all over the place. The moment you walk in you are watching yourself with a critical eye! You see yourself from every angle. I see myself grimacing as I lift a few pounds over my head. I see the flabby flesh. I say to myself, "Ernest, you used to unload boxcars, lifting one hundred pound sacks of sugar at a time. What has happened to you?" Sheepishly I must acknowledge that I just do not keep myself in shape by staying on a consistent exercise program.

Intimidated? Absolutely, but it is for my own good. Like Jesus said, if you do not use what you have, even what you have will be taken away from you.[1] This is true of both your physical life and your spiritual life. An hour's exercise does a body good, and an hour's prayer does your spiritual man a whole lot of good too. To get the best results at either the spa or prayer closet, a person should work up a routine that enables him/her to build up systematically what they have to work with. Follow a routine; be consistent in these important matters. You may not become the world's strongest man, or you may not become another Praying Hyde or George Mueller, but you will have the satisfaction of being a healthy, productive you!

Most people do not pray for an hour because they do

---

[1]     The principle is repeated so much, we dare not avoid it: Matthew 13:12; 25:29; Mark 4:25; Luke 8:18; 12:48; 16:10; 19:26.

not know how. They need a routine that will enable them to build up their spiritual faith muscles. My friend, that is why we have the Lord's Prayer. Let me lead you through an hour of spiritual exercise. You will wonder where the time went!

## Get Your Gear Together

Certain equipment will greatly enhance your times of prayer. You will need a Bible for Word-praying. Have paper and pen for taking notes of important thoughts that will come to you. Have an outline of the Lord's Prayer to help pace yourself through the time allotted. I particularly like Dick Eastman's nine points of focus which appeared in one of his monthly bulletins. I will use his format in sharing how my life and ministry have been shaped through Jesus' prayer. Hopefully the nine focuses of the Lord's Prayer will make your morning prayer time more inspirational and fruitful.[2]

Maintain a list of important prayer requests that can be presented at appropriate times. Also, if you are going to be a "world-class" prayer person, you need a good prayer map like the one supplied by Dick Eastman.[3] If you pray in the cold early morning in your living room, you may need a blanket to wrap around yourself! Now, let us begin!

---

[2]  Matthew 6:9-13. For excellent material on prayer contact Dick Eastman's *Change The World Ministries*, P.O. Box 5838, Mission Hills, California 91345. Another good source is Larry Lea's "Prayer Guide" from Church on the Rock, Box 880, Rockwall, Texas 75087.

[3]  In addition to a color-coded map of the more than 200 registered nations, a suggested list of seven nations and seven missionary agencies is given for each day of the month.

1.  A FOCUS ON WORSHIP...

    "Our Father which art in heaven"

    Concentrate attention on praising God for who He is.

2.  A FOCUS ON AUTHORITY...

    "Hallowed be Thy name"

    Sanctify, or "set apart" some of the names of our Lord in Scripture and apply them to circumstances.

3.  A FOCUS ON AWAKENING...

    "Thy kingdom come"

    Claim the "awakening" power of Christ's kingdom in your life, your family, and Christ's Body everywhere.

4.  A FOCUS ON EVANGELISM...

    "Thy will be done on earth as it is in heaven"

    Claim God's will in your life, family and the world-- always remembering, "God is not willing that any should perish"!

5.  A FOCUS ON PROVISION...

    "Give us this day our daily bread"

    Pray not only for personal needs--take time to feast in the provision of God's Word! (Learn to "pray the Word.")

6. A FOCUS ON FORGIVENESS...

   "Forgive us our debts, as we forgive our debtors"

   Time is needed to pray for a spirit of forgiveness, including the willing acknowledgment of past failures.

7. A FOCUS ON GUIDANCE...

   "Lead us not into temptation"

   Pray for guidance in specific matters, seeking God's direction to avoid temptation in all areas of life.

8. A FOCUS ON WARFARE...

   "Deliver us from the evil one"

   Boldly take authority against "the evil one" commanding his strongholds to crumble.

9. A FOCUS ON REJOICING...

   "For Thine is the kingdom and the power and the glory, forever. Amen"

   Conclude with a time of rejoicing in yet more praise!

## A Focus on Worship

Our Father which art in heaven. On the Nautilaus equipment I start on the weight machines that exercise the big leg muscles. "This gets the blood pumping," the young man said, "it's the best way to start."

Start your times of prayer with worship and praise. Leave the personal things until later, placing your whole attention on God. Begin with adoration! Strangely, this is sometimes hard to do, but this action glorifies God and lifts the person praying into an expectant, faith-filled state of mind. Try standing and lifting your hands to God.[4] Lift also your voice in magnification of the great God that has saved you. If spontaneous praise does not come easily to your lips, utilize the power-packed verses found in the Psalms. Take a passage and personalize it, such as Psalm 100:

I shout joyfully to you, oh LORD, and so does all
the earth.
I serve You with gladness;
I come before You Lord with joyful singing. . .
    Thank You, LORD, I bless Your name.
For You are good;
Your lovingkindness is everlasting,
And Your faithfulness is to all generations.

Allow your mind to revel in His great redemption. Thank Him for the precious blood of Christ that has purchased your salvation. Take several minutes for concentrating praise on the living God for who He is.[5] Let

---

[4]   1 Timothy 2:8.

[5]   Larry Tomczak suggests using a listing of the "ABCs of God's Attributes," by associating divine attributes with letters of the alphabet. *Divine Appointments*

your mind acknowledge and your tongue confess that God is both your Father and "our" Father in and through the Lord Jesus Christ. He is the God of all creation who is exalted above all things in the universe. Talk to God, and do not be afraid to verbalize your feelings in solid terms. When David cried out: "Bless the LORD, O my soul! O LORD my God, Thou art very great!"[6] he was doing just what we are doing-- verbally recognizing God for who He is.

The opening statement is like an invocation, it is God's own instruction on how we may gain a joyful entrance to His very presence. Notice that we do not approach the Almighty by calling Him "God," or "My God," but rather the personal, warm term "Father." Jesus clarifies for us that we are in intimate relationship that can best be described as that between a loving father and a grateful child. The pronoun "Our," explains Hebrew expert Brad Young, "means that no single individual has a monopoly on God, and that, as His followers, we have a responsibility to one another."[7]

## A Focus on Authority

**Hallowed be Thy name.** Adoration continues as the heart and mouth speak and sing of His greatness. Join with the angels and the living creatures in declaring His holiness: HOLY, HOLY, HOLY, is THE LORD GOD, THE ALMIGHTY,

---

(Ann Arbor, Michigan: Servant Publications, 1986), p. 127.

6    Psalm 104:1.

7    Brad Young, *The Jewish Background to the Lord's Prayer* (Austin, Texas: Center for Judaic-Christian Studies, 1984), p. 4.

who was and who is and who is to come.[8]

Holy, Holy, Holy, is the LORD of hosts,
the whole earth is full of His glory.[9]

Actually take words like this and prayer-read them aloud.
Sometimes I have walked back and forth in my living room,
holding the Bible in my hands and reading these words. Do
not mumble them, but speak them directly and forcefully to
your Father: "My Father, You are holy, holy, holy, You are
the LORD God, the Almighty." We, of course, cannot make
Him more holy, but our cry is an acknowledgment that He is
holy, and we declare it so that that holiness may find
expression through the exaltation of His name in our lives.

Our God has many names and attributes. Use them in
your opening prayer time. Let your mind revel in the majestic
meanings as your mouth makes audible confession: "You are
the Mighty God, You are the Living Lord, the Great I AM."

Declare His attributes: "You, oh Lord, are absolute
Love, You are Kind and Merciful, You are so Longsuffering."

Try taking a few minutes of doing nothing else but
praising and adoring His names and attributes! Take a few
minutes to recite the great miraculous acts of God recorded
in the Scriptures. One morning I began to do this and found
myself so inspired that I continued for forty-five minutes just
on the theme of God's greatness alone! Make it a practice to
open your prayer time with worship and adoration, for as
Harold Lindsell says:

> Adoration is the first and the highest form of
> prayer. In its simplest and finest form it is the
> worship and praise of God by one of His children.

---

8    Revelation 4:8.

9    Isaiah 6:3.

It consists in acknowledging God as God, in paying to Him the devotion of heart He requires of true worshippers....Adoration should be the first prayer uttered by devout lips except, perhaps, in moments of great crisis....When one can engage in serious prayer, in organized and regulated fashion, the place to commence is with adoration.[10]

## A Focus on Awakening

**Thy kingdom come.** Some theologians feel that the kingdom of God is the main theme of Jesus' teaching and ministry. This is hard to refute. Jesus seemed to have a wonderful sense of kingdom timing which apparently was born out of His times of prayer. For Jesus the kingdom was presently operating and yet there were still future ramifications of it that were to come. Brad Young reminds us that the "the Hebrew language emphasizes the *kind* of action and not the time" and suggests that the meaning Jesus had in mind here was "May you continue establishing your Kingship."[11]

Be very practical in praying this part of the prayer. "Oh, God, let me be under Your rulership this day. Let your kingdom find expression in and through me." Petition God to rule in your own personal life. I call out to God the names of my wife, my four children and their spouses, my four grandchildren, and assorted other relatives. I pray for our church staff by name. The city officials, the president, -- whoever makes decisions that affect the society. "Oh, God, King of the universe, let Your kingdom find expression in all of these areas!"

---

10   Lindsell, pp. 30, 31.

11   Young, p. 11.

Having prayed for myself to come under the kingdom (for several years), I can testify that such praying will indeed shape and affect your ministry. Such prayer releases the Holy Spirit to deal with those areas of your life where you may be "a few bricks short of a load." I have found the fire of such praying brings the dross to the surface quickly. Things for me, such as procrastination, criticism, and anger, have been identified and brought under kingdom authority more readily than before.

As we make these practical applications to prayer, one can see that it is necessary to settle into a time slot that will allow such amplification. This I urge strongly, of course, for a period of at least an hour, and the fact that such praying would be done the first thing each day would make a dramatic difference in the way that each day would unfold.

### A Focus on Evangelism

**Thy will be done on earth as it is in heaven.** I like Dick Eastman's statement: "No prayer can be answered out of God's will and no petition can be refused when offered in God's will."[12] The Apostle John said: "And this is the confidence which we have before Him, that, if we ask anything according to His will, He hears us."[13]

The third and fourth phrases concerning the kingdom and the will of God easily overlap. Their scope easily overlaps as well. Personally, I have no difficulty in praying for the hidden people groups of the world that have yet to hear the

---

[12]  Dick Eastman, *Change the World! School of Prayer* (Studio City, California: World Literature Crusade, 1976), p. C-7.

[13]  1 John 5:14.

Gospel of Christ and also praying for the spirituality of my grandchildren! God does not seem to have problems with the smallness or the greatness of our requests.

I like to use a prayer map, running my fingers over the nations of the earth, praying for them by name. My dear elderly mother used to pray for global missions in an interesting way. She would spread out a big world map on the floor and then walk, in stocking feet, over the nations praying for God to pour out His spirit upon them. I cannot help but feel that mother's modern adaption of God's word to Joshua has merit:

> Every place on which the sole of your foot treads, I have given it to you, just as I spoke to Moses.[14]

About two years ago the name of an Islamic nation in Africa started coming to my mind. I have prayed, wondering if I am supposed to go or if there is something that I should do. This particular nation is closed to the Gospel and has outlawed Christian evangelistic efforts. Recently we had a missionary to an Hispanic country with us. He told of how his people were beginning to get a world-wide vision, illustrating the point by mentioning a business man that was going to move to the Islamic country of my prayers and set up a business so that he might spread the Gospel! I consider this to be at least a partial answer to my prayer.

Once I read how A.B. Simpson, founder of the Missionary Alliance Church, had a guest minister staying overnight. Coming downstairs early the next morning, the guest found Simpson with his arms around a globe of the world weeping for the nations. At the time I thought that was a rather remarkable thing for Simpson to do, wondering if I would ever be so moved.

---

[14]     Joshua 1:3.

One day, however, as I was praying over the nations of the world, using a large globe in my church office, I unconsciously found myself holding the earth in similar fashion, crying out tears for God's kingdom and will to be wrought in the earth. The Lord had gradually apprehended my heart! For me early morning prayer has been the divine tool for enlarging my global vision to become a "world Christian."

One cannot pray this prayer continuously and seriously without being changed! When I pray for our local church, I ask God to help us be apostolic, prophetic, evangelistic, pastoral, and teaching.[15] This kind of praying for kingdom activity to be within and outgoing from the church must produce results. In our case it has kept our church mentally alert to foreign missions, and we have been able to start six other USA churches as well! It would not have happened, however, without the powerful objectives of Jesus' prayer working daily in our hearts.

## A Focus on Provision

Give us this day our daily bread. In a land where fast food restaurants abound, we find it difficult to pray this prayer with sincerity. It is actually a cry of acknowledgment that our Father is the source of supply for all our needs. I extend this prayer over my daily schedule. Whoever I expect to meet, decisions that must be made, all are brought under the provisions of this request. We are not begging, but we are following Jesus' teaching to bring our basic, daily needs to Him. Be specific, use names and places. Include even the unexpected interruptions that will undoubtedly take place.

Astounding as it may seem, we may in one moment deal with the advancement of the kingdom throughout the world,

---

15    Ephesians 4:11.

and then talk to Him in the next moment about the day-to-day matters of our personal lives. We may ask God to oversee our financial affairs. We may talk to him about a vacation or more suitable transportation. Continually affirm that your Father has the control of your life in His hands.

Money has become a massive idol, and the love of money is the root of all evil.[16] Praying this prayer will cause more to go into missions than personal frivolities. An amazing feeling of security will envelope your life as you trust Him for your daily provision.

## A Focus on Forgiveness

Forgive us our debts, as we forgive our debtors. The word "debts" here can refer to sins or trespasses, not just financial indebtedness. What does it mean to forgive? Remember this definition: to grant free pardon to a person who has offended you, to cease to feel resentment against or desire for revenge. Forgiveness deals with our emotional response toward an offender. We may not always have the legal authority to pardon an offense (as when a murder is committed), but we can always forgive. Forgiving a person is "clearing the record" with us and transferring the responsibility for any punishment to God. Forgiveness will make it possible for us to have the same openness toward him/her after the offense as we had before the offense.

I remember hearing the astounding true story of a Christian man whose wife was savagely attacked and sexually abused by another man. The woman died and her assailant was apprehended, jailed and sentenced to death. The lonely husband prayed for this murderer of his dear wife. He began to have a great desire to go to the prison and meet this man face to face. After repeated efforts he was finally allowed to

---

16    1 Timothy 6:10; Luke 16:1-15.

visit the prison. As the two men faced each other in the cell block, the Christian said, "I forgive you for killing my wife, just as Christ has forgiven me of my sin." As the truth of this honest confession gripped his heart, the condemned man dropped to his knees and accepted Christ as his Savior!

Kneeling seems the most appropriate posture for this prayer. Time should be allowed for God to impress your mind. I have been prone to ask hastily for forgiveness and simply assume that I have not had ought against anyone. Sometimes I know that I need to bring the names of certain people to God that I have disliked or held grudges against. Praying this prayer consistently has done wonders in helping me clear up the bad feelings.

Also, when you are free of guilt, and praying in the spirit of this request, God is allowed to work in the hearts of others. I have had three people come to me in the past three months seeking to make things right with me. One dear brother who had formerly attended our church had carried a heavy emotional attitude problem toward me for several years. He saw me in a public setting, came up to me and explained his problem. We resolved it, thank God, right on the spot. Praying this prayer continuously will help you forgive, and also help others to feel the freedom to come to you.

The other day while I was praying, rather grateful that I had nothing in my heart against anyone, the Lord showed me that my attitude toward a certain television evangelist was not right. At first I rejected the thought, but then when I actually lifted the man's name to God and began asking the Lord to help him, a new sense of release came to me. It is all right to have personal convictions, but judgment is still in His hands. Be at peace.


A Focus on Guidance

Lead us not into temptation. We know from James, the

first chapter, that God does not tempt anyone. Jesus is not telling us that God will lead us into temptation unless we pray that He will not. Rather, it is a prayer that God's saints will not be exposed to trials so severe that their loyalty to God may be undermined. "Keep me, O Lord, from any situation where I will discredit Your name or dishonor Your Word!"

This is the kind of prayer that requires urgency and sincerity. We are asking God not to allow us to be overwhelmed by a temptation, and therefore succumb to it. We are calling upon God to keep us from the snares of the enemy. "Father, do not let us be subjected to any temptation or trial which would destroy us, cause us to lose faith in You, or disobey Your will." Specifically ask God to keep you this day from doing anything that will discredit or dishonor His name, anything that would in any way bring reproach on the Gospel of Jesus Christ.

Do not stop there, take a few more minutes with this concept. "Lead us, oh Lord, in such a way that we can discern the satanic presence and purpose in every situation involving moral enticement, sinful seduction, suffering, persecution, or martyrdom."

This prayer acknowledges that we will be tempted, but our expectation is that through God's grace we will not yield to it. Jesus will help us: "For since He Himself was tempted in that which He has suffered, He is able to come to the aid of those who are tempted."[17] God prefers that we encounter evil and be delivered from it, rather than that He would deliver us from all encounters with it.[18]

If you are troubled with some addictive habit, do not be mired down by a faithless anxiety. Begin daily laying your hands on yourself and affirm strongly in prayer: "This body,

---

[17]     Hebrews 2:18.

[18]     Judges 3:4; John 17:11, 15; Luke 21:36; 1 Corinthians 10:13; Psalm 19:13, 14.

O Lord, belongs to You. I am a temple of the Holy Spirit. Purify and cleanse this temple! Release my mind and body from all destructive addiction." The habit will begin to yield to your insistent prayer, and soon it will go.

Fervently bring Jesus' suggested request to God each day. It does indeed break the power of temptation. You will find yourself maintaining spiritual vigilance much more easily. Discernment of evil intentions becomes commonplace. This prayer does indeed shape the attitudes and ministry of an individual.

## A Focus on Warfare

**Deliver us from the evil one.** As we come to the end of the Lord's Prayer, we petition for deliverance and request protection. Every prayer time should remind us to be alert to the schemes Satan may bring against us as we go about our activities of the day.

I like to mentally go through the armory mentioned in Ephesians 6. It is helpful to visualize the various pieces of armor, and deliberately ask God to clothe me with those spiritual attributes. "Dear Lord, let my mind be girded about with truth. Thy Word is truth. I am sanctified by Thy truth." Continue to "put on" the armor: the breastplate of righteousness, the shoes of peace, the helmet of salvation, the shield of faith, and the sword of the Spirit.

As you prayerfully ask for this protection, your spiritual sensitivities are strengthened. Paul said to "put on" the armor, and how else can it be done except through specific prayer?

Our enemy will come as a tempter, accuser, and adversary. He will attempt to lie, steal, kill and destroy. Our prayers will be particularly effective if they incorporate the following thoughts:

1.    Help me not to provide Satan with compromising,

embarrassing situations that allow him to do his evil work.
2. Give me wisdom to discern and avoid his traps.
3. Enable me to believe that God is my source for all things, and to walk with the same sureness that Jesus had because I know the Father.
4. Help me to be invulnerable because I want God's will to be uppermost in my life.
5. Develop in me a wholesome attitude about my body and mind which makes it difficult for destructive habits to form and work.
6. Let my world view and personal philosophy be that of God alone.

## A Focus on Rejoicing

**For Thine is the kingdom and the power and the glory, forever. Amen.** The great prayer closes with a doxology ( a hymn or form of words containing an ascription of praise to God).[19] The prayer began with praise and worship. Coming full circle we now conclude our prayer with worship. Every prayer should begin in praise and end in praise, because praise is the sum total of all true prayer.

These are the things that we ascribe to God in a doxology: power, riches, wisdom, might, honor, glory, blessing, dominion, greatness, victory, majesty, authority, and thanksgiving. Look up the passages mentioned in the footnote (19) and read these magnificent words as part of your prayers. Say the words in the spirit and intensity with which they were written.

"Amen!" expresses our confidence that God will honor

---

[19]    Some Scriptural doxologies: 1 Chronicles 29:11; 2 Chronicles 20:6; 1 Peter 4:11; Jude 25; Revelation 4:8, 11; 5:12, 13; 7:12; 11:17; 15:3-4.

our petitions. It means "May it be so." To add "Amen" to our prayer is like the judge striking his desk with the gavel, proclaiming, "Court adjourned." Consider ending a session of prayer by singing the hymn *Amazing Grace*, only substituting the word "Amen" continuously for the regular words.

I prefer to pray most of my time in the morning, and then pray just a few sentences before hopping into bed at night. I have always felt that my evening tiredness does not lend itself to important prayer. Here is a suggestion that has proven inspiring to me. Finish your day, not with requests, but with again praying the Lord's Prayer. This time, however, thank Him in each section of the prayer for the ways in which you have seen your morning prayers answered. Specifically mention in prayer the events of the day and the ways in which you perceive that God has helped you. Great peace will flood your soul as you realize afresh that His provision covers you just like the blankets cover your body.

## Variety Is the Spice of Life

It is a terrible shame for a Christian to lose out on his/her prayer life because of boredom or monotony. I am persuaded that God is a God of variety and surprises. If we will approach our prayer times with anticipation and faith, allowing the Spirit to inspire our minds, exciting things happen--and no two prayer times will be exactly alike. It is not necessary to plod through the phases of the Lord's Prayer in some wooden fashion. This was never the Lord's intention.

Although the concepts of Jesus' prayer should be kept in mind, it is possible to be impressed by the Holy Spirit to pray for people, jobs, missions, whatever, in a spontaneous way that you perceive is being directed of the Lord. We can learn to pray out of our hearts and with the inspiration of the Holy Spirit. We should not be uncomfortable with following a set format either. Utilize the tools mentioned previously, but do not feel bound to them. We are real children entering the presence of the true and living God. We are coming before Him in intercession, prayers, petitions, praise, and worship. This is what God wants, for us to come to Him in prayer:

> 'Then you will call upon Me and come and pray to Me, and I will listen to you. And you will seek Me and find Me, when you search for Me with all your heart. And I will be found by you.' declares the Lord.[20]

---

[20]     Jeremiah 29:12-14.

C H A P T E R

# The High
# Priestly Prayer

## The Missing Key

"Where is that Key?" I asked myself.

Invariably when I am in a hurry my keys seem to disappear. On this occasion I was not only in a hurry, but I was very concerned about retrieving some important papers from our safety deposit box at the bank. The key in question was to that box. Because of its importance the key had been put in a special place--and I had forgotten the place!

The safety deposit box key is not an elaborate key for such an important duty. Compared to my collection of large, colored, ornate, and odd-shaped keys, this flat key with just a few grooves is deceptively plain. There is, nevertheless, no other key in my possession of greater importance; it alone will fit the second lock on the safety deposit box, and it is specifically registered at the bank in my name. The box cannot be opened without it.

Each deposit box has two locks. One lock is opened by

the bank key, and the second by the depositor's key. The bank teller takes both keys into the vault, then inserting and turning the keys simultaneously, pulls the safe's door open. She then pulls the box out of the safe and hands it to the depositor. The depositor now has the freedom to do whatever he wishes with the contents.

As I rushed about searching for my key, I realized that I was running out of time. I had to go! I felt that somehow the problem would be solved at the bank. The teller knows me, knows my name, knows that I live nearby, and certainly trusts me since she knows I am a minister! I felt rather self-assured as I approached the bank counter.

The friendly teller greeted me like a long-lost friend. (Things were going well!) As I began to sign in at the counter, I casually, laughingly mentioned that I could not find my key. Instantly I knew I was in trouble. The teller became all business (no smiles!).

"Reverend Gentile," she said, "I cannot open your box without that key. You must have the key!"

"But I've looked for it and can't find it," I replied with sincerity. "Couldn't you possibly open it for me?"

In no uncertain terms she informed me that the box could not be opened, and that it would be a major project to bring in the safe expert to change the lock and make a new key.

"Why don't you go home and look again," she said.

Seriously worried now, and feeling frustrated and deflated, I turned away and walked slowly to my automobile. After much mental anguish and frantic search, I found the key and returned to the bank ( a nervous wreck!). Cheerfully (as though nothing had happened!) the teller took my key, inserted it with the bank key, turned my key, opened the door, drew out the box, and (with a smile!) placed it in my hands. What a relief! And...what a lesson.

Heaven's Vault

Heaven is like a bank vault that is filled with wonderful things that are legally ours. Access, however, is gained only with the simultaneous cooperation of two spiritual keys: (1) God's sovereign will, and (2) man's faithful prayer in accordance with that will.

God can and will do wonderful, miraculous things. He is sovereign and all powerful. He is the mighty God and there is nothing He cannot do.[1] Why, then doesn't this perfect, powerful God just go ahead and run His universe without involving me and my prayers?

Today's Church is beginning to understand the reason for prayer, even though it is mind boggling: God has chosen only to accomplish His will in the earth through the prayers and intercessions of His people.[2]

The key of God's will is now available for any legitimate situation. When a person, then, has the matching, sympathetic key of proper prayer and faith, the sovereign power of God is released to do His will in that given situation. Heaven's vault is open to those who faithfully pray in the will of God! God and man working together become the two matching keys that release the impossible. The Apostle John confirms this concept when he says:

> And this is the confidence which we have before Him, that, if we ask anything according to His will, He hears us. And if we know that He hears us in whatever we ask, we know that we have the

---

[1] Note Jeremiah 32:17, 27; Luke 1:37; 18:27.

[2] Paul Billheimer develops this theme admirably in his inspiring book *Destined for the Throne* (Ft. Washington, Pennsylvania: Christian Literature Crusade, 1975).

requests which we have asked from Him.[3]

Jesus brought out this very thought in three intriguing statements, using keys in one of them to illustrate His point. First, consider Matthew 16:19 in the New American Standard:

I will give you the keys of the kingdom of heaven; and whatever you shall bind on earth shall have been bound in heaven, and whatever you shall loose on earth shall have been loosed in heaven.

The followers of Jesus will function as doorkeepers who act in accordance with the will of heaven; therefore we will follow the instructions already predetermined by heaven's King.[4] Charles B. Williams brings this out in his translation of the above verse: "...whatever you forbid on earth must be what is already forbidden in heaven, and...what is already permitted in heaven"[5]

When we pray in the will of God, claiming in faith what already is determined in heaven, we will find answers to our prayers. Another reference is mentioned in Matthew 18:18:

Truly I say to you, whatever you shall bind on earth shall have been bound in heaven; and whatever you loose on earth shall have been loosed in heaven.

---

3    1 John 5:14, 15.

4    The heathen King Nebuchadnezzar was made to "recognize that it is Heaven that rules" and God is "the King of heaven" (Daniel 4:26,37).

5    Williams adds a footnote: "Pf. pass. part., so things in a state of having been already forbidden." *The New Testament in the Language of the People* (Nashville: Holman Bible PUblishers, 1986), p. 47.

Finally, John 20:23 records this statement of the risen Jesus to the disciples gathered in a locked room:

If you forgive the sins of any, their sins have been forgiven them; if you retain the sins of any, they have been retained.

## The Prayer of Our High Priest

Jesus prays as a high priest in John 17: first, as one who is about to offer sacrifice (Himself); and second, as the high priest described in Hebrews 7:25 and Romans 8:34 who stands before the throne of God making intercession for us.

If there was ever a prayer that could be considered as a model "key" that conformed to the will of God, surely this would be it. The deep, unselfish piety, the unabashed confidence of Jesus, the unusual insights--all factors combine to make this glorious prayer the finest of all prayers. Hebert Lockyer, in his study on the prayers of the Bible, says of this prayer that "We have now come to the Holy of Holies in the New Testament."[6]

I have read this chapter dozens of times--on my knees, seated at a desk, silently, audibly, privately, publicly. I have attempted to outline the chapter, noting the oft-repeated words, etc., and each of these studies has yielded great benefit. The most profitable aspect of this prayer to me, however, is understanding what the prayer is and why it occurs in this period of Jesus' life.

We have all heard sermons closed with a prayer. John 17 is just that. It is the closing prayer of a farewell speech. Jesus has just given one of His most profound sermons (called His "Final Discourse") in chapters 14, 15 and 16. This

---

6    Herbert Lockyer, *All the Prayers of the Bible* (Grand Rapids: Zondervan 1959), p. 227.

amazing prayer is the conclusion of that deeply spiritual message. Jesus has shared some of His greatest thoughts in a special communion teaching with His disciples; then, He moves into direct communion prayer with His heavenly Father--allowing them to listen in! Although praying on earth, Jesus lifts the disciples into the heavenlies. I like the comment of A.B. Bruce: "He speaks to God as if He were already in heaven, as indeed He expressly says He is a little farther on: 'Now I am no more in the world.'"[7]

The prayer of Jesus is not silent intercession. Although a prayer of wonderful intimacy between Son and Father, the prayer is spoken aloud. The prayer is instructional as well as intercessory. With His eyes lifted to heaven and His words addressed to the heavenly Father in intercession, Jesus also instructs by example the listening disciples. In a sense Jesus prays to an audience, for He wishes His concepts to make a lasting impression on the disciples. He gives them concepts that they must pray here on earth after He is gone, and He illustrates the nature and concerns of the perpetual intercession that will engage Him at the Father's right hand as their high priest.[8] Eleven rugged, childlike men listened to their Master's instructional prayer, and then one of them recorded those sterling words for the benefit of the Church in all ages.

As He prayed before them, He shared the perfected fruit of what He had learned about prayer during His many early morning sessions in the Father's presence--and He showed them the basic content of His continued prayer when He would ascend back to the Father in heaven.

---

7      A.B. Bruce, *The Training of the Twelve* (Grand Rapids: Kregel Publications, 1971, reproduced from the Fourth Edition, 1894 by A.C. Armstrong and Son), p. 449.

8      Hebrews 7:25, 26.

We teach our children to pray by allowing them to observe our posture and sincerity while listening to the words we speak. Small children at the dinner table will frequently want to lead in prayer, and we should let them, but it is also important that they hear adults pray on a regular basis. The precepts of prayer and faith are communicated to the child even as the parent prays directly to God. This is exactly what Jesus was doing in John 17, just as He had done in Luke 11:1-4.

### The Savior's Heavenly Intercession

This is the greatest thought that I know about this prayer: Jesus' prayer in John 17 is an anticipation of, an explanation of, the coming intercession which He would perform in heaven at the Father's right hand. This prayer is a bridge between His earthly prayers of agony and the coming heavenly prayers of glory. The development of Jesus' personal prayer life has become so synchronized at this point with the will of the heavenly Father, that He now prays in perfected form the climactic prayer of His earthly ministry--so perfect indeed that it becomes the link between His earthly and heavenly ministries. The listening disciples hear in basic form how the Son of God will be praying in heaven! Jesus as the ascended high priest will pass into the heavenlies, there to engage in a heavenly intercession that will make Him the mediator between God and men.[9] Here are some significant verses:

> Since then we have a great high priest who has passed through the heavens, Jesus the Son of God, let us hold fast our confession. For we do not have a high priest who cannot sympathize with our

---

[9]  1 Timothy 2:5; also, Hebrews 8:6; 9:15.

weaknesses, but one who has been tempted in all things as we are, yet without sin. Let us therefore draw near with confidence to the throne of grace, that we may receive mercy and may find grace to help in time of need.[10]

Hence, also, He is able to save forever those who draw near to God through Him, since He always lives to make intercession for them.[11]

For Christ did not enter a holy place made with hands, a mere copy of the true one, but into heaven itself, now to appear in the presence of God for us.[12]

Christ Jesus is He who died, yes, rather who was raised, who is at the right hand of God, who also intercedes for us.[13]

And if anyone sins, we have an Advocate with the Father, Jesus Christ the righteous.[14]

---

[10]   Hebrews 4:14-16.

[11]   Hebrews 7:25.

[12]   Hebrews 9:24.

[13]   Romans 8:34.

[14]   1 John 2:1.

CHAPTER

# The Eternal Intercession

## Jesus Prays for Me

Jesus has prayed for me, and He still prays for me. What a thought! As a child I envisioned Jesus the mediator presenting to the Father all of my little, material needs. Sometimes halting, sometimes embarrassed, I would struggle with what Jesus was actually saying to the Father about me and my needs. As a youth I wondered if somehow heaven was like some gigantic telephone switchboard with Jesus frantically plugging in certain calls to the Father's throne while holding other calls. This whole business of Jesus presently "interceding" for me was perplexing, to say the least! I could understand that Jesus did pray for me during His earthly ministry, but it was difficult for me to relate Jesus' present interceding with prayer. Somehow I knew that John 17:20 included me:

I do not ask in behalf of these alone, but for those

also who believe in Me through their word.

Now, thank God, I boldly come before the throne, no longer bogged down with trifles, but praying in the broad, sweeping terms of the great priestly prayer of Jesus. I know that He is neither a frail human telephone operator or some massive, complicated computer system. My Jesus is somehow, wonderfully and mysteriously, a living part of the Godhead, and He is indeed personally concerned about me and my problems. I am encouraged to read that when Stephen, the first recorded Christian martyr, was dying, he saw Jesus standing (apparently giving great attention to Stephen's situation):

> But being full of the Holy Spirit, he gazed intently into heaven and saw the glory of God, and Jesus standing at the right hand of God; and he said, "Behold, I see the heavens opened up and the Son of Man standing at the right hand of God."[1]

### The Three Parts of the Prayer

Jesus' prayer in John 17 is the bank's key, because it so perfectly expresses the will of the Father. My prayer (in tandem with and running parallel with that prayer) is the secondary key which enables the Holy Spirit (as the bank officer) to open the vaults of heaven for this hopeful child of God.

I am impressed that Jesus prayed first for Himself. My personal tendency has been to pray for others, feeling that it was selfish and almost sacrilegious to be overly concerned with personal needs. But this magnificent prayer begins with a bold,

---

[1]    Acts 7:55,56.

direct request to the Father for personal glorification[2] His request at first seems uncomfortable, but through prayerful meditation one soon realizes that without being "glorified" by the Father (being enabled to do the will of God so that God will receive all the glory) we are not really capable of glorifying God.

As we pray to the heavenly Father, let us continually rejoice in the glorification of Jesus, for this is the theme which best pleases the Father. Pray as well for your own glorification, for it is in this process that Jesus is truly exalted and glory given to God.

Note that the remaining seven prayers are for the Church. Jesus seemed to feel that the Church is of uppermost importance to God. Many times we spend long periods of prayer concentrating on "sinners" and their problems and conversion. Jesus prayed for His followers, not for the world.[3] He prayed fervently for those "given" to Him.[4] Jesus is concerned "that the world may believe",[5] but that seems to be the expected end result of the other prayers. An excellent insight on this is provided by A.B. Bruce:

> The design of Jesus in making this statement is not, of course, to intimate the absolute exclusion of the world from His sympathies. Not exclusion, but concentration in order to eventual inclusion, is His purpose here. He would have His Father fix His special regards on this small band of men, with whom the fortunes of Christianity are bound up.

---

2    John 17:1,5.

3    John 17: 9,11,15,20.

4    John 17:2,6,11,12.

5    John 17:21.

He prays for them as a mother dying might pray exclusively for her children,--not that she is indifferent to the interest of all beyond, but that her family, in her solemn situation, is for her the natural legitimate object of an absorbing, all-engrossing solicitude. He prays for them as the precious fruit of His life-labor, the hope of the future, the founders of the Church, the Noah's ark of the Christian faith, the missionaries of the truth to the whole world; for them alone, but for the world's sake,--it being the best thing He can do for the world meantime to commend them to the Father's care.[6]

### His Seven Requests for the Church

1. **Keep them in Thy name.**[7] All of these requests reflect the concern of a shepherd for His sheep. Here Jesus cries for their preservation through their knowledge of Himself (His name and His person being one). When we pray for a fellow believer to be kept in God's name, be assured that our prayers are certainly in tune with the way Jesus is presently praying in heaven.

2. **That they may be one.**[8] This is the most famous of the seven requests; in fact, the popularity of this majestic

---

[6]     A.B.Bruce, *The Training of the Twelve* (Grand Rapids: Kregel Publications, 1971, reproduced from the Fourth Edition, 1894 by A.C. Armstrong and Son), pp. 455,456.

[7]     John 17:11.

[8]     John 17:11,21,22,23.

request has so captured the minds of Christians everywhere that we hardly notice the other prayers. This is, of course, a prayer for unity among His followers--a cry that finds particular sympathy in heaven at this time. This request is reminiscent of Psalm 133 which extols the excellency of brotherly unity.

**3. That they may have My joy.**[9] We mainly know Jesus as a man of sorrows, but He was also a man of great joy.[10] The meaning of this request is clearly seen in the Amplified Bible:

> And now I am coming to You. I say these things while I am still in the world, so that My joy may be made full and complete and perfect in them--that they may experience My delight fulfilled in them, that My enjoyment may be perfected in their own souls, that they may have My gladness within them filling their hearts.

**4. Keep them from the evil one.**[11] This is not just evil things, but rather "out of the power of" the devil. This presents us with an excellent expression when praying for others. This is still Jesus' wish![12]

---

[9]    John 17:13.

[10]    See Hebrews 12:2; John 15:11; 16:22; Jude 24.

[11]    John 17:15.

[12]    Note Matthew 6:13; 1 John 2:13; 3:12; 5:18,19; John 13:2,27.

148 ♦ AWAKEN THE DAWN!

5. **Sanctify them in the truth.**[13] As people believe the truth, respond to the truth, walk in the truth, they create the atmosphere in which "the Spirit of Truth" operates best. We are set apart for God's purposes, we are made holy, we are best enabled to do the will of the Father--when we have the sanctifying power of divine truth working in us.

6. **That they be with Me where I am, in order that they may behold My glory.**[14] This is indeed a desire of Jesus. He longs to have us with Him. He longs to share His glory. He presently intercedes that we may be with Him.

7. **That the love wherewith Thou didst love Me may be in them, and I in them.**[15] In a sense, this prayer is that we disciples would be obedient to His instructions in John 15:9,12:

Just as the Father has loved Me, I have also loved you; abide in My love....This is My commandment, that you love one another, just as I have loved you.

Jesus states it as a command in John 15:17:

This I command you, that you love one another.

Jesus did not just assume that His commandment would be followed. He prayed--and apparently He expects us to pray-- that Christians would be filled with Jesus' love. His most famous statement on the subject in John 13:34,35 should be in our prayers because we know that it is even now in His:

---

13    John 17:17.

14    John 17:24.

15    John 17:26.

A new commandment I give to you, that you love one another, even as I have loved you, that you also love one another. By this all men will know that you are My disciples, if you have love for one another.

## Peter and Job: Something in Common

Two very interesting verses are dropped into the Gospel record which give insight into Jesus' deep concern for the disciples as well as how He prayed for them individually then and how He intercedes now:

> Simon, Simon, behold, Satan has demanded permission to sift you like wheat; but **I have prayed for you**, that your faith may not fail; and you, when once you have turned again, strengthen your brothers.[16]

It is not apparent in our English translations that the first "you" is in the plural in the Greek text, indicating Satan's desire to sift all the disciples. When Jesus says, however, "I have prayed for you," He is speaking directly to Peter and the "you" here is in the singular. Notice the wording of these verses in the Amplified Bible:

> Simon, Simon (Peter), listen! Satan has asked excessively that (all of) you be given up to him--out of the power and keeping of God--that he might sift (all of) you like grain, [Job 1:6-12; Amos 9:9]. But I have prayed especially for you [Peter] that your [own] faith may not fail; and when you yourself have turned again, strengthen and establish

---

[16]    Luke 22:31,32.

your brethren.

Satan suddenly appears as an adversary to Jesus' disciples, particularly Simon Peter. Jesus, aware of happenings in the spiritual realm, is clearly alert to this hostile desire to take over His followers and submit them to such severe trial and testing that their faith and constancy will be destroyed. Jesus becomes the advocate of His followers, particularly praying for Peter.

This concept of Satan desiring to put the disciples to the test is reminiscent of the opening chapters of the book of Job. To understand how Jesus prayed for Peter and how He presently prays for the Church, it is important to understand the story of poor, tormented Job.

Behind the narrative of a pathetic, desperately ill man is a spiritual story that boggles the mind. Job's trials and sickness were not the result of his own foolishness or lack of faith but rather the result of spiritual forces locked in a war of cosmic proportions. God in His infinite wisdom allowed Satan the devil to present his own devious, diabolical requests. As Satan rambles across the earth, he seeks to wreck havoc in the lives of human beings, particularly those who serve the living God. Job is dutifully serving the Lord, unaware that behind the scene of natural happenings, a plot is brewing in the spiritual realm which could mean his total destruction. This report given in Job, when linked to how Jesus prayed in Luke, gives us amazing insight for understanding life--and how to pray effectively!

Do not mistake the discourse between God and Satan as mere wrangling, as if they were two carnal businessmen haggling over a piece of real estate. God is proud of His people,[17] and He does not hesitate to boast of them to Satan--even though He knows that Satan will immediately challenge the spirituality of any commended saint. He knows

---

[17]   Hebrews 11:16.

that if His troubled child will trust Him even through the trials which Satan is allowed to bring, God will be glorified, the saint will be strengthened spiritually, and Satan will be defeated.

It almost seems that Job's trial is precipitated by God's own provocative question:

> Have you considered My servant Job? For there is
> no one like him on earth, a blameless and upright
> man, fearing God and turning away from evil.[18]

Satan argues that any man so protected by God would serve Him. God responds by saying that Satan may do anything he wishes with Job's wealth, but that the man must not be harmed. Throughout the devastation of his belongings Job holds true to God, and this causes God again to boast of His servant to Satan. Then Satan asks to touch the man's body. God says, "Go ahead, only don't take his life."

God has allowed Satan an audience with Himself periodically, and God allows this ancient adversary to make provocative statements and even demands about God's people. We see it clearly in the book of Job. God will not allow Satan to afflict this man unless Satan first asks and obtains permission. Satan may do his worst, but always within prescribed boundaries.

This same adversary continues his evil work in the New Testament time. Jesus, with prophetic insight, perceives that Job's story is being reenacted as Satan claims the right to sift Simon Peter like wheat.[19] You get the full dynamic of Satan's request when you look at more than one translation of this verse:

---

18      Job 1:8.

19      Luke 22:31.

Satan hath desired to have you--King James
Version
Satan demanded to have you--Revised Standard
Version

Satan has claimed the right to sift you all like
wheat--James Moffatt Translation

Satan has received permission to test all of you--
Today's English Version

Satan has been given leave to sift--New English
Bible

Although God allows Satan to make his requests and
afflict woes upon the people of God, God is not really incited
or provoked into such permission. Jesus understands that this
is standard operating procedure at this present time. God will
be best glorified, Jesus knows, through this process of allowing
Satan to do his worst. The Church is meant to triumph under
the most trying and difficult circumstances--not the best. Jesus
knows through His communion with the Father that His
ancient foe is bent on destroying the faith of Peter and the
other disciples.

How does Jesus pray? He intercedes with the Father
that Peter's faith will not fail, and that he will be enabled to
strengthen the brethren. This is the essence of Jesus' present
intercession in heaven.

Much of Jesus' earthly praying, I am persuaded, was that
the faith of the disciples would not fail the testings and trials
that would be inevitable. That is how He prayed for Peter,
and surely this is the essence of the seven prayers of John 17.
Now in heaven, Jesus Christ continues His great concern for
the faith of His followers, and any of our prayers that flow in
this great channel of concern will undoubtedly find special
attention. Remember this great statement of Hebrews 13:8

when you approach the Lord in prayer:
Jesus Christ is the same yesterday and today, yes and forever.

CHAPTER

# Gethsemane:
# Last Morning of Prayer

### Garden of the Oil Press

The time together for their Passover meal was finished, and the high priestly prayer prayed. Now, to close their activities in that place, they sang a hymn.[1] There seemed to be only one place for Jesus to go at this moment...the garden called Gethsemane.

Directly east across the Kidron Valley from the great marble walls of the Temple was the Mount of Olives, and within the olive grove there was a garden or enclosure. Jesus probably led the disciples out the gate north of the Temple, then He would head down through the Kidron Valley toward that secluded spot that had so often been a refreshing retreat for Him and the disciples. It seems plausible that during this walk, perhaps as they came to the outskirts of the orchard,

---

1   Matthew 26:30. This is a time for singing a Scriptural prayer like verses from Psalm 115 to 118.

Jesus explained to Peter and the disciples how Satan wished to sift them like wheat. These were heavy thoughts for tired, sleepy, bewildered men. At last they arrive at Gethsemane (meaning "oil press"), a name that suddenly conveys an ominous, foreboding, even prophetic significance.

Feeling weary from the long day, and comfortably fed from the Passover meal, eight of the disciples easily responded to Jesus' invitation to sit and wait near the entrance. Possibly a covered place containing an oil press provided them some shelter. We know from the Gospel record that it was a small enclosed property, probably a garden having a variety of fruit trees and flowering shrubs. Jesus resorted to this place often,[2] not only for rest and sleep, or for a private gathering with the twelve disciples, but this was preeminently a place of prayer, a meeting place with the Almighty. Jesus told the eight to remain, "while I go over there and pray."[3]

## The Need to Prevail in Prayer

All Christians will pray at certain times under ordinary conditions, and this is how it should be; we are blessed and helped through this type of rather commonplace, unremarkable praying. Times do arise, however, in the course of human events when uncommon, extraordinary praying is called for! Unfortunately the practice of prevailing prayer is neither understood or practiced nearly enough by today's Christians.

It seems important to interrupt the story of Gethsemane momentarily to stress the importance and necessity of prevailing, phenomenal prayer. This book could have easily

---

2    Luke 22:39, "as He was in the habit of doing" (Williams Translation).

3    Matthew 26:36.

ended on an emotionally high point, giving the impression that simply going through the mechanics of early morning prayer or praying for an hour each day will make you a bubbling, vibrant Christian.

To be honest, however, to finish the message of Jesus' earthly prayer life, we must look at His experience of prayer in the garden and while hanging on the cross. This, my friend, is the highest, most notable example of extraordinary prayer. Although the physical story must be told in rather foreboding terms, the fact is that Jesus shows us during His darkest times of trial the rarest and most glorious possibilities of prayer. I am glad that this is part of the story, for I have found that every life will have dark moments of personal sadness, and we must know that we each are capable of extraordinary prayer at such times. Mature Christians must also be objective in their world-view--understanding God's dealings with the world as well as the satanic influences exercised on it. I like Wesley L. Duewel's statement about great praying:

> Prevailing prayer is prayer that pushes right through all difficulties and obstacles, drives back all the opposing forces of Satan, and secures the will of God. Its purpose is to accomplish God's will on earth. Prevailing prayer is prayer that not only takes the initiative but continues on the offensive for God until spiritual victory is won.[4]

Duewel stresses that in prevailing prayer you prevail: over yourself, over Satan, and before God. This is top level praying! It is from such prayer that glorious victories are won.

One of the greatest ordeals of my pastoral life was the five-year period in which a lawsuit hung like a dark cloud over

---

4   From one of my favorite books on prayer: Wesley L. Duewel, *Touch the World Through Prayer* (Grand Rapids: Zondervan, 1986), p. 194.

my personal life and our church. It was a difficult, emotional time for me, and I do not think that I could have held up under the strain if I had not already established the discipline of daily, early morning prayer. I am not at liberty to discuss the details of all that transpired, but I can tell you that prayer became vital to my life at that time. In a most dramatic fashion, the suit was resolved on the morning of the day in which we were to go to trial "to the mutual satisfaction of all parties involved." During the five-year period I prayed much, but I think all of that praying was necessary to bring me to a certain point of extraordinary prayer, just several days before the resolution. I was deeply concerned about going to court with a fellow Christian,[5] and I found myself asking God with deep pleading to let nothing happen that would discredit Him, the Spirit of Truth, or any of His people (including the plaintiff). It was at that moment--for me--that something wonderful happened, and I knew that finally I had touched upon that which was sacred to God. A deep peace settled into my soul that has not left me since. To God be the glory.

As we return to Gethsemane let us rejoice again for the magnificent triumph of the Christ in the garden and on the cross. His agony was turned to ecstasy as He persevered in the will of God: "who for the joy set before Him endured the cross, despising the shame, and has sat down at the right hand of the throne of God."[6]

### Sorrow and Heaviness

With ever-increasing burden, Jesus labored forward into the dark garden. Three disciples--Peter, James, and John-- follow Him, dropping to the ground a discrete distance from

---

5    1 Corinthians 6:1-8.

6    Hebrews 12:2.

the sorrowful praying Christ. Three times He will agonize in extraordinary prayer as the disciples sleep.

Jesus asked for their help in prayer:

And He took with Him Peter and the two sons of Zebedee, and began to be grieved and distressed. Then He said to them, "My soul is deeply grieved, to the point of death; remain here and keep watch with Me.[7]

His impassioned plea went unheeded, however, as their heavy eyelids locked in sleep.

Why such heavy emotion? It seems only moments ago when Jesus was lifting them up to heaven itself with His glorious priestly prayer. He spoke at that time with such assurance of victory, but now He is "very distressed and troubled."[8] His soul is sorrowful and deeply grieved to the point of death. He seems to go from a mountain top of spiritual ecstasy to a dark valley of despair, agony,and doom. Is He so fearful of dying? Have not other men, less brave or virtuous than He, accepted death more willingly, died more bravely, showed their confidence in God's purpose more perfectly? It would seem so to those who know not the grand mystery of it all.

Jesus was to die physically, yes, but more than that He was to die bearing the full weight of spiritual guilt for every man. His death was more than a mere expiring of natural life, a cessation of breath. The Christ now entered the arena of final conflict with Death itself, the last enemy of man and the great reaper of lost souls. A paragraph by Alfred Edersheim describes so well this spiritual dimension that it seems

---

7    Matthew 26:37,38.

8    Mark 14:33.

unnecessary to attempt saying it in any better form:

> But what, we may reverently ask, was the cause of
> this sorrow unto death of the Lord Jesus Christ?
> Not fear, either of bodily or mental suffering: but
> Death. Man's nature, created of God immortal,
> shrinks (by the law of its nature) from the
> dissolution of the bond that binds body to soul.
> Yet to fallen man Death is not by any means fully
> Death, for he is born with the taste of it in his soul.
> Not so Christ. It was the Unfallen Man dying; it
> was He, Who had no experience of it, tasting
> Death, and that not for Himself but for every man,
> emptying the cup to its bitter dregs. It was the
> Christ undergoing Death by man and for man; the
> Incarnate God, the God-Man submitting Himself
> vicariously to the deepest humiliation, and paying
> the utmost penalty: Death--all Death. No one as
> He could know what Death was (not dying, which
> men dread, but Christ dreaded not); no one could
> taste its bitterness as He. His going into Death was
> His final conflict with Satan for man, and on his
> behalf. By submitting to it He took away the
> power of Death; He disarmed Death by burying his
> shaft in His own Heart. And beyond this lies the
> deep, unutterable mystery of Christ bearing the
> penalty due to our sin, bearing our death, bearing
> the penalty of the broken Law, the accumulated
> guilt of humanity, and the holy wrath of the
> Righteous Judge upon them. And in view of this
> mystery the heaviness of sleep seems to steal over
> our apprehension.[9]

---

9      Alfred Edersheim, *The Life and Times of Jesus the
       Messiah* (Grand Rapids: Eerdmans, 1950), Vol. II,
       pp. 538,539.

Thus, Jesus bravely enters the "olive press" of the Father's good will that the best oil of personal dedication might be extracted.


## His Last Morning of Prayer

This is Jesus' final, climactic time of early morning prayer.[10] In a sense this is the prayer that will eclipse all of the other prayer times combined, for employed in this intense, magnificent intercession will be the total learning experience of the Son of Man. Through the years of His ministry Jesus has obediently walked in the principle of Isaiah 50:4,5. Morning by morning He has awakened to the Father's presence and voice. He now reaches the pinnacle of His life's fulfillment as He prays His last morning prayer.

On this morning, however, He is obviously not awakened by the Father, because the unrelenting events allow Him no time for sleep. It is a time of destiny and prophetic fulfillment.

All that Jesus has learned as an "awakened disciple" is summoned now to His aid as His soul bows beneath the weight of human life's greatest challenge: to do the will of the Father even when that action means the loss of all other things near and dear. The sinless Man is to die for the sins of the world. He who knew no sin is to take our sins upon Himself.[11] The penalty of sin and rebellion against God

---

10    Generally we think of the Gethsemane prayer as an evening or night-time prayer. It was, in fact, in the wee hours of the morning of the day of His crucifixion, possibly about 2 a.m.

11    2 Corinthians 5:21; Colossians 2:14.

must be paid, for "the wages of sin is death."[12]

Jesus' apparent hesitancy and shrinking from the coming death was not craven fear or cowardice. This was not some terrible dread of physical pain or the awful prospect of being deserted by friends and associates. It was the battle of human will surrendering to divine will. He who was the Son of God was also the Son of Man.

---

[12] Romans 6:23. That debt is now paid, and whoever will repent of his sins and call on Christ may be saved, coming under the pardon granted by the Father to all who acknowledge--believe in and trust in--Christ's death for us.

CHAPTER

# Drinking the Awesome Cup

## Is There a Gethsemane for Me?

None of us, thank the Lord, will ever experience or repeat Jesus' Gethsemane experience exactly. After all, the destiny of the whole human race and God's plan of salvation rested on what He did. He faced death in the ultimate sense--the horror of separation from the Father. Was He willing to undergo this experience, trusting His total outcome into the hands of the Father? Yes, He did this for us. This glorious victory in prayer was necessary only once, and this was achieved wondrously by the Christ of God.

Each of us will, however, have times in life when the human will, set on its own destructive course, must face the will and purposes of God. Such times of anguish will be our own "garden of the oil press" experience, and we will be bettered because of them. These times of heavy intercession may involve the human will ascertaining the will of God in heaven and then prevailing in prayer--regardless of personal feelings--until that divine will is accomplished.

## The First Prayer: "Abba! Father!

The Gethsemane prayer progresses through three phases of increasing intensity. Each segment reveals Jesus in greater struggle as He seeks the will of the Father concerning "the cup" which He must drink.[1]

Jesus faces the challenge of His Crucifixion with all that it entails. His death on the cross looms before Him as a dreadful cup, and to drink this cup is to submit fully His will as the Son of Man to the full purpose of the heavenly Father. The cup before Him becomes the battle of the human will to do obediently the will of God. A victory here will be not for Jesus only, but for all men everywhere. I have already quoted Hebrews 12:2 which tells us that all of this was endured "for the joy set before Him." Sorrow and joy wrestled within Him. His joy as the Son of God must be reconciled to the sorrow of Him who was also the Son of Man.

We can scarcely comprehend the power of His prayer or the burning flame of His determination which fed the prayer. As Son of God He knows His hour is at hand to die for the sins of the world--for this cause He came into the world, and now He would die and leave the world.[2] As Son of Man, feeling all of our infirmities, weaknesses, and inhibitions, Jesus struggles in a mighty wrestling match reminiscent of Jacob's grand struggle with an angel.[3] As with Jacob, the awesome battle of Jesus is more with the inner man than some outside force; it is the battle of the human will.

---

1    Matthew 26:39.

2    John 16:28.

3    Genesis 32:24,25; Hosea 12:3,4.

The struggle is reflected in His posture of prayer: He "fell on the ground."[4] He "fell on His face."[5] Perhaps the closest experience to this type of prayer is a woman's travail in birthing a child. Prayer warriors through the centuries have known and understood this kind of prayer as "soul travail."

Although emotionally distraught, Jesus nevertheless employs the loving title "Father." Matthew records "O My Father," and Luke uses just "Father." Mark, however, gives the significant "Abba! Father!"[6] Certainly no Jewish rabbi would use such a term in common prayer, let alone at such a serious time as this. It was considered too personal, too intimate, too familiar, inappropriate, and forward. To say "Abba" to God was (in their teaching) to reduce God down to a common, conversational level--and such was deemed impossible in the thinking of the Jewish leaders of that day.

For Jesus, the use of "Abba!" in this prayer was the conditioned response of one who had come to realize that God is to be known in a personal, intimate, and familiar way. At this anxious moment in Gethsemane, His truest and most sincere understanding of God surfaces in expression. Even in the moment of most excruciating agony, Jesus bonds to God as heavenly Father.

## The Second Prayer: An Angel Appears

Returning to the disciples after His first period of prayer, Jesus admonishes them (particularly Peter) to watch and pray that they not enter into temptation (or, a trial that would cause them to discredit the Lord). This is the same thought

---

4   Mark 14:35.

5   Matthew 26:39.

6   Mark 14:36.

166 ♦ AWAKEN THE DAWN!

mentioned in the Lord's Prayer, and we see it now as a life-principle built into Jesus' character.

Discouraged, Jesus steps away from the disciples about the distance of a stone's throw. There in the dark recesses of the garden He falls to His knees in anguish, again asking the Father if His will might be done without His drinking the awesome cup.

At this point of the story we find a starting verse in Luke 22:43:

> Now an angel from heaven appeared to Him, strengthening Him.

The angel "appears" to Jesus. There must have come a great surge of emotional confidence as Jesus realized the Father's concern, but I cannot doubt that there was also a literal, although perhaps momentary, surge of energy as the angel touched and assured Him. On another momentous occasion, after He had fasted forty days in the wilderness and been subjected to Satan's temptations, Jesus had heavenly visitors. Exhausted in the wilderness and depleted of all physical energy, having used His total remaining reservoir of strength to overcome the last temptation, Jesus was "ministered to" by angels.[7]


### The Third Prayer: Sweat Like Gouts of Blood

It was after the angel's appearance that the final segment of prayer took place. Again, only Luke describes the intense scene:

> And being in an agony He prayed more earnestly: and His sweat was as it were great drops of blood

---

[7]     Matthew 4:11.

falling down to the ground.[8]

The question is often asked, "Does this mean that Jesus actually sweat blood while He prayed?" Truthfully, we do not know for sure. Both the linguistic problems of the text as well as the medical verification of such a phenomenon are open to question. It really is not necessary to believe that His sweat was bloody to understand the objective of Luke's record.

Luke's point is simply this: the third prayer, following the strengthening by the angel, shows an earnestness that defies description. Although the early morning hours are cool and the ground moisture-ridden, the Son of God prays with such fervency that His body reacts in the most extreme physiological manner possible.

Sweat pours from His body, not as tender perspiration, but as spurting blood would flow. His sweat, bloody or not, rolled from His body like gouts of blood. There is an article in *Herald of His Coming*, in which Stephen Olford's book is quoted in describing the experience of Evan Roberts, the leader of the Welsh Revival of 1904-5:

> During a morning meeting which Evan Roberts attended, the evangelist pleaded that the Lord would "bend us." The Spirit seemed to say to Roberts, "That's what you need, to be bent." And thus he described his experience:
>
> "I felt a living force coming into my bosom. This grew and grew, and I was almost bursting. My bosom was boiling. What boiled in me was that verse: 'God commending His love.' I fell on my knees with my arms over the seat in front of me; the tears and perspiration flowed freely. **I thought blood was gushing forth.**" Certain friends

---

8    Luke 22:44, King James Version.

approached to wipe his face. Meanwhile he was crying out, "O Lord, bend me! Bend me!" Then suddenly the glory broke.[9]

Luke's desire is to show us that before Jesus' mind was set at ease--before His will capitulated to that of the Father, before assurance flooded His mind that all was settled and right--He physically and emotionally plumbed the depths of human exertion and despair. This He did for us.

Then, rising from His last morning prayer time, Jesus awakens the disciples. A mob with flashing torches and clanking swords arrives to take Him captive, led by a betrayer with seared conscience. Jesus meets His tormentors with a majestic confidence, clothed with power that comes only from time spent in the Father's presence.

There He stands with human ropes binding His body, but His soul is free indeed! He knows what God's will is, and He moves forward with eager anticipation to see it brought to glorious climax. Death holds no fear now, and Jesus with joy sets Himself to finish His course and put an end to man's last enemy.[10]

---

9    Stephen F. Olford, "When the Fire of God Falls," *Herald of His Coming.* August 1989, p.3. Taken from his book, *Heart-Cry For Revival.*

10   Acts 2:23, 24; 2 Timothy 1:10.

CHAPTER

# The Glorious Climax: Cries from the Cross

### His Greatest Moment

When Jesus taught us to pray, "and lead us not into temptation,"[1] He was sharing a tremendous insight that was based not only on prophetic revelation but also the practical out-working of the concept in everyday life situations. Jesus, of course, was not teaching us to pray for or expect a life free from temptation or trial; He knew that these things when properly handled only sharpen our faith. The word "temptation" can mean not only moral enticement, but it can mean "trial" or "test" in the sense of suffering, persecution, or martyrdom. These things come, but by praying daily for the strength to resist being overwhelmed by such temptation, the Christian fortifies himself and assures future victories.

The personal result of praying this thought daily has been very profound in my life. God truly seems to honor our

---

[1]     Matthew 6:13.

intentions of serving Him, and when the enemy sweeps in upon us or natural calamities strike, there is a reserve power waiting to carry us through! I find that one can "store up prayer." If our prevailing prayers are active and continuous, we build a solid account in heaven's bank which can be drawn upon in time of trouble. Fortunately, the Lord gives us "breathing space" between trials, and it is then that our consistent prayers become like savings deposits. since this has been true in my limited experience, I can easily conceive that this sustaining power was wondrously present in the suffering Christ as He prayed on the cross.

We Christians sing praises continuously for the dazzling victory of Christ on the cross. The rugged cross that was meant to be a torture rack and an instrument of death has instead become the symbol of God's abounding grace and Christ's greatest glory. Wesley Duewel states this profoundly:

> Have you realized how total was Christ's victory at Calvary? It was a victory for us because Jesus took our place, bearing our sin on the cross. He paid the price for our redemption. He fulfilled the Old Testament prophecies and all the Old Testament types. Every sacrifice for sin from Adam onward was accepted by God upon the condition of the final, perfect, and holy sacrifice of Christ on the cross. So every sacrifice accepted by God from a repentant sinner was like one more debit, one more promissory note which Jesus guaranteed to pay. Praise God! On the cross He paid it all! Calvary was an eternal victory for whoever wills to receive it (Revelation 22:17).[2]

---

[2]    Wesley L. Duewel, *Touch the World Through Prayer* (Grand Rapids: Zondervan, 1986), p. 105.

Jesus spoke words from the cross, during His agony, of profound emotional and spiritual significance. Our concern will focus on the three prayers He directed to the heavenly Father.

## Father, Forgive Them

Jesus' first words from the cross were, "Father, forgive them; for they know not what they do."[3] Thus He begins (and later ends[4]) His vigil on the cross conscious of His heavenly Father and His will that must be done.

As soldiers gambled for His garments at the foot of the cross, while religious bigots hurled accusations at Him, as the disciples scattered and malefactors on either side taunted him--Jesus forgave them all. In the prayer He had taught the disciples, the one phrase which merited His personal commentary was "forgive us our debts, as we also have forgiven our debtors."[5] Right at the end of the prayer He said:

> For if you forgive men for their transgressions, your
> heavenly Father will also forgive you. But if you do
> not forgive men, then your Father will not forgive
> your transgressions.[6]

I cannot help but think now of how Jesus awakened morning by morning to be taught by the Father and to be

---

[3] Luke 23:34.

[4] Luke 23:46.

[5] Matthew 6:12.

[6] Matthew 6:14,15.

given words of comfort for the weary.[7] Jesus is able to pray this magnificent prayer of forgiveness from the cross because of the Father's grace that has been worked in Him morning by morning. He has come to see people as the Father sees them!

This same attitude worked powerfully in the early Church as well. Stephen, the first recorded martyr, fell on his knees as he died, crying loudly: "Lord, do not hold this sin against them!"[8]


## My God...Why?

At the conclusion of a strange darkness that has fallen over the whole land, He cries, "My God, My God, why hast Thou forsaken Me?"[9] This anguished cry (unlike the other two prayers) does not use the warm, familiar "Father," but rather "God" in a startling, cold, hortatory manner. Has He been abandoned by God in this most awful hour?

At first, this prayer seems like a shout of utter desolation. This is, rather, the cry of Jesus the Son of Man, voicing in behalf of all people the hopelessness of the sinner dying in his sin without a Savior. The strange darkness filling the land through that afternoon of the Crucifixion was a graphic sign sent by the heavenly Father to give dynamic confirmation in the natural realm to that which occurred in the spiritual realm.

The words in this prayer are found in the opening sentence of Psalm 22. The description of the Crucifixion scene is so accurate that one cannot help but wonder if this is in fact recorded history rather than prophecy.

---

[7]     Isaiah 50:4.

[8]     Acts 7:60.

[9]     Matthew 27:46; Mark 15:34.

Charles Spurgeon makes this appropriate comment in his opening remarks on this chapter:

This is beyond all others THE PSALM OF THE CROSS. It may have been actually repeated word by word by our Lord when hanging on the tree; it would be too bold to say that it was so, but even a casual reader may see that it might have been.[10]

I feel that the Psalms were very real to Jesus. I know this is a very personal conclusion, but it seems so true from my own experience. It is difficult to pray day after day (for any length of time) without involving God's Word--particularly Psalms. The marvelous way in which the Psalms pour spontaneously from His lips testify of their careful use in years of personal devotion and training. It was as though the cross was the high accomplishment for which every morning of prayer had prepared Him.

### Father, Into Thy Hands

His last words on the cross are confident and vibrant, "Father, into Thy hands I commit My spirit."[11] He has completed the task given Him by the Father. He does not cry out, "I am finished!" No, instead He declares, "It is finished!" A glorious surge of fulfillment and sense of victory whelms up within Him. That which has been a daily prayer for personal needs and sustenance, now becomes the ultimate experience of dependency on God.

---

10 Charles H. Spurgeon, *The Treasury of David* (Byron Center, Michigan: Associated Publishers and Authors, Inc., 1970 reprint), Vol 1, p. 365.

11 Luke 23:46. Note Psalm 31:5 uses these words also.

174 ♦ AWAKEN THE DAWN!

He dies a victor! Although wounded and forsaken by men, He who dies from the serpent biting His heel crushes with that same heel the awful head of sin.[12]   With His death, Death dies.[13]   Having done all, He commits Himself into the Father's hands, the ultimate act of faith of Him who is the supreme example of prayer.

---

[12]    Genesis 3:15.

[13]    Note 1 Corinthians 15:54-57.

# Epilogue

Thank you so much for letting me share with you my insights and experiences in prayer. I hope that you are more encouraged to pray on a daily basis than ever before.

Now, how do you feel about early morning prayer? Personally, I am more convinced than ever, but sometimes there are problems...

This morning my alarm sounded with such ferocity at 5:15 that I literally bounded out of bed. But...it had been a late night, so maybe I could skip morning prayer today? I crawled back into bed. My goal was to get up for six o'clock prayer. At 5:45 my wife said, "Ernest, this is not like you, aren't you going to get up?"

I have missed before, but my beloved companion has never made any comments! I rallied my strength and got up. I could not stay in bed on the day that I finished my book on early morning prayer! I used every argument in this book to get out of bed! Finally, I rolled out of bed and headed for prayer.

Needless to say, the prayer time, as always, was great--just a wonderful time with the Lord. Jesus, the most famous pray-er of all time hit the nail squarely on the head when He said: "the spirit is willing but the flesh is weak!"[1]

Daily prayer gives me a high vantage point from which to view our global world problems. I think that I now understand better why Jesus walked with such sure confidence in the Father's will; prayer enabled Him to keep His feet on the ground--but His mind on a spiritual plane. Jesus seemed to see things from God's perspective. Prayer will do this for all of us. The necessity of genuine prayer seems so obvious.

So...we all know that we should pray, but I doubt that any of us pray as much or as well as we would like. I am very concerned that our failures to pray might become blankets of condemnation that will smother any further attempt to pray.

It is true that to be effective in prayer we do need to be as disciplined as athletes in competition, people seeking weight loss, or salesmen seeking sales. Determination! Prayer will soon be forgotten if we listen to the body or look at our circumstances. Yes prayer does take effort.

On the other hand, if we miss times of prayer, we must not be discouraged. I like the advice given by Jack McAlister, one of the great prayer warriors of this generation. Jack served as president of World Literature Crusade for thirty-three years, and has a wealth of background in prayer. I listened intently as he spoke at a recent prayer workshop.

He had already surprised me by saying that his goal was to pray for two and a half hours each day as a tithe of his time. But he was quick to say that sometimes he missed his prayer time, but he has learned not to condemn himself for the time missed. He advised us to do the best we can with each day, appreciating whatever time we can give for undivided attention to the Lord. I agree with him that our motivation for daily prayer should not be from the approach

---

1     Matthew 26:41.

of "duty" or "I should." These attitudes will make us fail! Our motivation must be from "the joy of being with Him."

Consistent daily prayer--particularly early morning prayer --will transform your life. So many wondrous things have happened in my life during the past few years because of this simple discipline, that I would feel guilty for not sharing this glorious treasure. By God's grace determine to be as consistent as you can in daily seeking the Lord, as early as you can.

Know this! If you will arise early each morning to seek the living God, you will not be alone. In your time zone there will be thousands of others calling out to the heavenly Father for the evangelization of the nations and the renewal of the Church.

Arise to...Awaken the Dawn!

# Bibliography

An Unknown Christian, *The Kneeling Christian.* Grand Rapids: Zondervan, 1986 (reprint of a classic). 125 pp.

Billheimer, Paul. *Destined for the Throne.* Ft. Washington, Pennsylvania: Christian Literature Crusade, 1975.

Bounds, E.M. *The Best of E.M. Bounds.* Grand Rapids: Baker, 1981. 231 pp.

Cho, Paul Y. *Prayer: Key to Revival.* Waco: Word, 1984. 177 pp.

Duewel, Wesley L. *Touch the World Through Prayer.* Grand Rapids: Zondervan, 1986. 255 pp.

Eastman, Dick. *No Easy Road.* Grand Rapids: Baker, 1971. 128 pp.

Eastman, Dick. *Change the World! School of Prayer.* Studio City, California: World Literature Crusade, 1976.

Eastman, Dick. *The Hour that Changes the World.* Grand Rapids: Baker, 1980. 174 pp.

Hallesby, O. *Prayer.* Minneapolis: Augsburg, 1931. 176 pp.

Hybels, Bill. *Too Busy Not to Pray.* Downer's Grove: InterVarsity, 1988. 156 pp.

Keller, W. Phillip. *A Layman Looks at the Lord's Prayer.* Chicago: Moody, 1976. 155 pp.

Lea, Larry. *Could You Not Tarry One Hour?* Lake Mary, Florida: Creation House, 1987. 191 pp.

Lindsell, Harold. *When You Pray.* Grand Rapids: Baker, 1969. 182 pp.

Lockyer, Herbert. *All the Prayers of the Bible.* Grand Rapids: Zondervan, 1959. 278 pp.

McGaw, Francis. *John Hyde: The Apostle of Prayer.* Minneapolis: Bethany, 1970 (reprint of a classic). 68 pp.

Muck, Terry. *Liberating the Leader's Prayer Life.* Waco: Word, 1975. 203 pp.

Murray, Andrew. *The Prayer Life.* Grand Rapids: Zondervan, 1988 edition. 111 pp.

Steer, Roger. *George Mueller: Delighted in God!* Wheaton: Harold Shaw, 1975. 320 pp.

White, Reginald E.O. *They Teach Us to Pray.* New York: Harper and Brothers, 1957. 204 pp.

Young, Brad. *The Jewish Background to the Lord's Prayer.* Austin: Center for Judaic-Christian Studies, 1984. 46 pp.